**Books are to be returned on or before
the last date below.**

Reorganizing primary classroom learning

Nigel Hastings and
Karen Chantrey Wood

Open University Press
Buckingham · Philadelphia

Open University Press
Celtic Court
22 Ballmoor
Buckingham
MK18 1XW

email: enquiries@openup.co.uk
world wide web: www.openup.co.uk

and
325 Chestnut Street
Philadelphia, PA 19106, USA

First Published 2002

A catalogue record of this book is available from the British Library

ISBN   0 335 20730 8 (pbk)   0 335 20731 6 (hbk)

Library of Congress Cataloging-in-Publication Data
Hastings, Nigel.
  Reorganizing primary classroom learning / Nigel Hastings and Karen
  Chantrey Wood.
    p. cm.
  Includes bibliographical references and index.
  ISBN 0-335-20731-6 – ISBN 0-335-20730-8 (pbk.)
    1. Classrooms–Planning. 2. Elementary school facilities–Planning.
  3. Classrooms–England–Planning–Case studies. 4. Elementary school
  facilities–England–Planning–Case studies. I. Title: Reorganizing primary
  classroom learning. II. Wood, Karen Chantrey, 1958. III. Title.

  LB3325 C5 H37 2002
  372.16′21–dc21

                                                      2001059104

Typeset by Graphicraft Limited, Hong Kong
Printed in Great Britain by St Edmundsbury Press, Bury St Edmunds, Suffolk

Contents

Acknowledgements

This book is about primary schoolteaching, is intended for primary schoolteachers and could not have been written without them. We are grateful and indebted to the teachers and headteachers – some of whose ideas, work and vision we have attempted to describe in the central part of this book – who welcomed us into their schools and classrooms, generously gave us their time and agreed to publication of accounts of their work in the belief that other schools, teachers and children might benefit. While responsibility for all that is written here rests with us, credit for the benefits that others derive from reading these pages belongs to these teachers.

Introduction

This is a book about the organization of primary classrooms. In fact, at its simplest, it is a book about classroom furniture, about how tables and chairs are arranged. Expressed like this, it hardly seems a topic warranting a modest leaflet, let alone a book. Why on earth would such a seemingly marginal and trivial issue as the arrangement of furniture in primary school classrooms be worth a publisher's investment, our time in writing and, perhaps of more immediate interest to you, your time in reading a whole book about it?

Our answer to this question lies in the fact that the conditions in which we ask children to work in primary school classrooms have a significant and generally unrecognized influence on their attention and learning. More than this, our argument is that the orthodox practice, especially in England but also elsewhere, of young children sitting in groups around tables makes learning unnecessarily difficult for much of the time. In other words, our case is that the way we expect children to sit in schools makes a real difference to their learning. Consequently, our superficially improbable thesis is that the arrangement of classroom furniture is not a marginal or trivial issue because it affects children's daily experience, learning and attainment throughout their primary school careers and has consequences that endure well beyond those early years.

These are not just speculative propositions. They rest on and are justified by a body of classroom research indicating that:

- there is a mismatch between the rationale for classroom organization and the teaching that actually goes on;
- rearranging classroom tables and chairs to support learning has a significant and worthwhile impact on children's attention and on levels of distraction;
- using classroom organization in a strategic manner and changing it for different purposes is a practicable option within most classrooms.

The last of these points is especially important. Research relating to the first and second claims has been reported and its implications considered in several publications in recent years. A further account is provided in Chapters 1 and 2, but Chapter 3 reports the outcomes of a project in which we tried to identify and describe the practices of teachers who arrange children's workspaces strategically. These cases are not offered as models of good practice, although all have impressed us, but to illustrate how practice can develop to mitigate the adverse consequences of some aspects of currently normal classroom practice.

No two classrooms are the same in architecture, furniture and facilities, let alone in their teachers' and children's skills and purposes. For this reason alone, none of the practices we describe can be borrowed as a whole package. However, these case studies can serve as a good source of ideas and, if you are a primary teacher, as inspiration to 'have a go', and to try enhancing the quality of learning in your classroom by adding seating organization to your professional repertoire.

Every now and then, primary classroom seating hits the newspaper headlines. The episode usually begins with a modest conference paper or research report attracting the attention of an education correspondent, but the 'news' quickly spreads. National tabloid newspapers in particular, but also radio and television stations, like to run stories on the issue, judging it to be of interest to their readerships and audiences. And they are probably right. Everyone has been to school and most adults are, have been or expect to be parents of school-aged children. However, it is not the detail of the research and its implications that attracts journalists' interest but what different seating arrangements seem to represent. In fact, it is not classroom seating *per se* but two particular seating arrangements – rows and groups – around which journalists sense that a good story can be built. These are not seen as just two configurations of furniture: they are taken to be the standards or emblems of two opposing and irreconcilable factions or camps.

Beliefs about what makes 'good teaching' and a 'good school' are often held with conviction and argued with passion. But passionate convictions can lead to polarization in debate and quickly render well considered and well informed discussion nigh on impossible. This is no better, or more frequently, illustrated than in pronouncements and less frequent exchanges on the merits of 'traditional' and 'progressive' methods. Twenty-five years ago, few would claim to support 'traditional' teaching methods without being abused as 'reactionary', 'authoritarian' and 'interested only in teaching subjects, not children'. In the last 15 years it has been 'progressive' teaching that has been subject to comparable abuse and parody as 'trendy' and 'wishy-washy', with 'progressive teachers' characterized as 'leftover lefties', 'bearded-wonders' or 'barefoot, sandal-wearing, wholemeal, hippies' with patronizing and low expectations for children, an enthusiasm for non-competitive sport and a tendency to talk of 'sharing' a great deal.

The interesting thing about all this unedifying and seemingly continuing tendency to view primary teaching as being available only in these two, equally silly versions, is that you don't tend to hear teachers themselves arguing in these ways. They rarely describe themselves as 'traditional' or 'progressive'. However, they and others working within education are conscious that the wider community is at least familiar with these slogans and, informed by politicians and some parts of the press, may classify teachers in these terms. But how might a parent, for instance, decide which of the two types their child's teacher is? Many features of a teacher's practice, and perhaps of their manner and appearance, will be taken as cues, but some seem more salient than others. Among the most prominent and significant seems to be the layout of their classroom.

The moment you walk into a primary classroom, you see the layout of its furniture. Long before noticing displays, resources or clues as to the curriculum and the quality of children's attainment, you notice the furniture. From this alone, a great deal more may be inferred through a widely-held and seemingly deep-seated set of associations between the appearance of a classroom and the beliefs and practices of its resident teacher. In short, a classroom arranged so that children sit in rows facing the front is assumed to be the classroom of a 'traditional teacher', while a classroom arranged so that children are seated around groups of tables is generally, though perhaps now less strongly, associated with 'progressive teaching'. It is precisely this link that drives, and is strengthened by, the occasional flurries of interest in classroom organization among journalists, for whom a clear polarization is enormously appealing, especially when it can be identified with the major political dimension of Left versus Right.

The association of seating in rows with 'traditional teaching' and the political Right, and of group seating with 'progressive teaching' and the political Left has the effect of making rational consideration of the relative educational merits of different ways of arranging classrooms difficult. The issue too easily becomes political and ideological. For the individual classroom teacher, conscious that parents and possibly headteachers, advisers or inspectors may hold these associations, the prospect of changing from established practice is daunting. To arrange your classroom in a manner that differs from the orthodox does not only invite questions about your educational rationale. It risks categorization and condemnation on political grounds.

It is against this background that this book is written. Our aim is to provide teachers, headteachers and those whose work is to support and advise them with accessible accounts of how current practice has developed, of research revealing relationships between classroom organization, teaching and learning and of the work of teachers who have developed ways of using classroom seating to better effect. As well as information, however, we hope that these pages will provide schools and teachers who want to improve children's experience and learning with an additional source of confidence to try new approaches. It is certainly time we used evidence to inform professional decisions on organizing classrooms for learning and broke free of the political and ideological associations that too often render discussion of possible modes of classroom organization frustrating, fractious and fruitless. The purpose of this book is not to advocate a particular form of classroom organization: it is to argue a principle – classroom learning should be supported by the environment in which it takes place.

Part 1
Primary classroom organization: rhetoric and research

1 | Good practice and primary classroom organization

Primary classrooms in developed countries tend to look pretty much the same. They differ in size and shape, in the number and height of the windows, in their decoration and state of repair, in the quality of resources and displays and in the number of children who work and endeavour to learn there. However, the presence of plenty of chairs and tables of a certain height, a black or whiteboard, books, posters and other stored resources, and maybe a few computers, distinguish primary classrooms from all other familiar spaces. The classroom furniture tends to be arranged in one of two basic forms, with children sitting either facing in the same direction or at grouped tables facing one another. In the UK, group seating is common, as it is in many North American classrooms, and is generally accepted as being good practice. In mainland Europe, practices vary a good deal, although there appears to be a move in some countries away from rows to groups. Elsewhere, in Russia and India for example, rows remain the norm (Alexander 2000) – as they were in UK classrooms until the mid- to late 1960s, when practice changed.

Back in 1963, the Conservative government's Minister for Education, Sir Edward Boyle, commissioned an inquiry into primary education from the Central Advisory Council for Education. Its report, entitled *Children and their Primary Schools* (Plowden 1967) but better known as 'The Plowden Report' or simply 'Plowden' after its chairperson Lady Plowden, was published in 1967 and received by the then Labour government's Minister for Education, Anthony Crossland. Since then, Plowden has served as a landmark in primary education. On one side was 'traditional' primary education, in which children were taught as whole classes and typically sat in rows. On the other side grew the 'progressive' era in primary education, characterized by changes to the curriculum, to teaching methods and to classroom organization, as well as by a belief in the need for education to engage with children as individuals. Whether quite such marked changes in classroom practice ever really took place at all, let alone astride the Plowden Report, has been questioned (e.g. Galton *et al.* 1999), but it is certainly often held that they did. It is also generally held that, for good or ill, the Plowden Report was substantially responsible for the direction and character of primary practice over subsequent decades, especially by those who have been critical of practice in UK primary schools since the early 1970s.

The strange thing about the popular and professional understanding of the Plowden Report and of its impact on teaching is that the report actually says very little about how teachers should teach. Of its 1252 paragraphs, just 7 are concerned with classroom practices and *teaching* does not even warrant an appearance in the index. The relevant section begins by noting changes that were already underway in primary schools:

> In the last 20 years schools have provided far more individual work, as they have increasingly realised how much children of the same age differ in their powers of perception and imagery, in their interests, and in their span of concentration. The more obvious this becomes, the less satisfactory class instruction seems.
>
> (Plowden 1967, para. 754)

Endorsing this reduction in the proportion of time that teachers were spending teaching the whole class, though still seeing an important role for some whole-class teaching, the same paragraph continues by highlighting the value of one-to-one teaching and advocating its continuing development. But the report also recognized a logistical problem:

Teaching must often be individual, though other children will look on, and often learn in the looking. The varying interests of older children and their differing ability and knowledge mean that they too ought to be taught as individuals both for reading and mathematics. Sharing out the teacher's time is a major problem. Only seven or eight minutes a day would be available for each child if all teaching were individual.

(Plowden 1967, para. 754)

For the Plowden committee, individual one-to-one teaching seemed to be the ideal learning context, as only in this situation could teaching be finely tuned to match the individual child's needs and understanding. The problem was that the basic organization of the primary school was, and in Plowden's view should remain, the teacher and a class, recommended to be no larger than 30. The simple mathematics of dividing one teacher's time across 30 children and the recognition that, while a teacher is working with one child all the others are without their teacher, seem to have led the committee to its compromise. Better than teaching the class as a whole, though less educationally beneficial than one-to-one teaching, teachers could move between teaching *groups* of children who are 'roughly at the same stage':

Ideally they might be better taught as individuals, but they gain more from a longer period of their teacher's attention, even though it is shared with others, than they would from a few minutes of individual help. This is particularly true of a group of children who have reached the same stage in reading and computation. A group of this kind should be formed for a particular purpose, and should disappear when the purpose is achieved.

(Plowden 1967, para. 755)

Leaving for now the resonance of this recommendation with recent developments in the teaching of literacy and numeracy in English primary classrooms, it is important to note that, for Plowden, groups were primarily a context for active teaching of a limited number of individuals, at a similar level of attainment, and a necessary compromise on the ideal of teaching individuals.

The report's recommendations were, therefore, that schools and teachers should try to increase the proportion of time that children are taught as individuals and as members of small groups, with the implication that whole-class teaching should decline in prominence. Team teaching was seen as one way in which two or three teachers, working together, could create situations where, while one or even two work with individuals or groups, the other, if not actively teaching, could at least manage the remainder of the combined classes in their work.

Although these practices were already established in some schools by the mid-1960s, the emphasis that Plowden placed on the merits of teaching groups of children and, to a lesser extent, on children working in collaboration, made it sensible for schools to arrange classrooms to support these activities. The report itself made no explicit mention of seating arrangements, but its advocacy of teachers working with groups seems likely to have accelerated the move from rows as the standard arrangement for classroom desks to the now familiar and orthodox practice of children sitting in groups of four to eight around all four sides of a square or rectangular surface. This transition was all but complete in English state schools by the early 1970s (Bealing 1972).

Lady Plowden's committee took 3 years to complete its work. Nearly 30 years later, the 'Three Wise Men' were given just a few weeks over Christmas 1991 to provide their recommendations on primary teaching, following press coverage of an evaluation of Leeds Education Authority's Primary Needs Programme (Alexander 1991), including a BBC *Panorama* programme. The three, appointed by Kenneth Clarke, Secretary of State for Education and Science, were Robin Alexander, Director of the Leeds evaluation project; Jim Rose, Her Majesty's Chief Inspector (HMCI) and, seemingly as a late addition, Chris Woodhead, who was then Chief Executive of the National Curriculum Council (NCC) and only later became more widely known following his appointment, as a successor to Jim Rose, as HMCI. Their brief was more limited than Plowden's and they were able to call on a body of research evidence on primary classroom teaching developed over the previous 20 years, the like of which simply did not exist in the 1960s when the Plowden committee began its work. Their task was: 'to review the available evidence about the delivery of education in primary schools and to make recommendations about curriculum organization, teaching methods and classroom practice appropriate for the successful implementation of the National Curriculum, particularly at Key Stage 2' (Alexander *et al.* 1992: 5). But it was not only the availability of research evidence and a more restricted brief and time scale that distinguished the contexts of Plowden's and the Three Wise Men's work. In the intervening years, education had moved to the foreground in politics, local education authorities (LEAs) had been heavily criticized and their powers reduced, the governance of schools had been transformed, a National Curriculum and national assessment system had been introduced, teachers' contracts had been revised and tightened and radical changes to the nature and frequency of inspections were about to impact. In short, education had become a major issue in party politics.

Although evidence from research on primary classroom practice was available to the working group of three, as with research evidence in all fields of inquiry it required interpretation and was neither completely consistent nor able to sustain many incontestable conclusions. But the issue was not just about evidence. Accounts of the work of the committee of Three Wise Men provided by Alexander as an insider (Alexander 1997), and by Galton (Galton *et al.* 1999) are both fascinating and disturbing in highlighting how the drafting of their report appears to have been influenced by outcomes that had, to some degree, been predetermined. Indeed, when publicly announcing that he was establishing the working group and its brief, the Secretary of State was understood by the press also to be making clear that its conclusions would be that 'trendy teaching' was to end and that 'traditional teaching' was to be revived in primary schools.

Whatever the background and whatever arguments took place in the drafting, it is clear that the working group did make substantial use of available research evidence. Like Plowden, their report, *Curriculum Organisation and Classroom Practice in Primary Schools* (Alexander *et al.* 1992), also conceptualized primary teaching in terms of individual, group and whole-class teaching activities, not least because much of the relevant research had investigated primary teaching in these terms. Briefly stated, the report's conclusions were that primary teachers had been devoting too much time to teaching individuals and making insufficient use of whole-class teaching. However, the report makes little mention of teaching children gathered together in groups for that purpose, as Plowden had recommended. Rather, its comments on groups focus on children working together *as a group*, whether or not the teacher is present. Observing, like many before, that although primary children generally sit *in* groups, but rarely work *as* groups, the authors note the heavy demands that planning and managing collaborative group work place on teachers' time and skills and the difficulties that arise if either is not done well.

So, to distil the essence of these two reports' ideas on primary classroom teaching, both considered and made recommendations on the use of individual, group and whole-class teaching and both encouraged a change in the balance perceived to be operating in schools at the time. Plowden sought greater individuation in both the curriculum and in teaching while, 25 years later, the Three Wise Men suggested that teachers were spending too much time engaging with individual children and that differences between children and their individual needs had been disproportionately emphasized. Plowden urged a more limited and selective use of whole-class teaching, while the Three Wise Men concluded that 'In many schools the benefits of whole class teaching have been insufficiently exploited' (Alexander *et al.* 1992: 35). As for the use of groups, the two reports had different emphases. For Plowden, a group is a good context for teaching, in that it enables teachers to respond to some of the needs of individuals while at the same time reducing the inevitable neglect of others arising from a focus on individuals. On the issue of children working together as groups, Plowden offered little substantial comment. Within the 1992 report, groups were considered mainly in terms of children collaborating in learning and of the teacher's role as manager of a class comprising groups working in this way. The only reference to teachers actively working with groups was cautionary: 'Teachers also need to be very careful in their investment of time between groups' (Alexander *et al.* 1992: 30).

Against this background, it is interesting to note a different emphasis again in the documentation supporting the National Literacy and Numeracy Strategies (NLS and NNS) implemented across primary schools in England from 1998, which provided teachers with guidance not only on curriculum matters but also on the organization of their teaching. Both strategies place considerable emphasis on whole-class teaching and on teachers actively working with small groups. One-to-one interaction is not prominent in either.

Two aspects of this brief history of ideas about the use of individual, group and whole-class teaching are important because of their relevance to the main concerns of this book. First, the way teaching is conducted would seem to have implications for how a classroom might be organized, yet although Alexander *et al.* make an oblique reference to the possibility that group seating may not be suitable for all learning tasks (1992: 29), neither of the reports makes any explicit recommendations on the physical layout of classrooms. This differs from popular expectation for, as we noted earlier, the Plowden Report is often viewed as having initiated, endorsed or promoted group seating as a replacement for the traditional rows of desks. Second although evidence played a significant part in the generation of the Three Wise Men's report, it seems that it was also informed by convictions held independently of the evidence. And so answers to educational questions will, to some degree, always remain, since judgements about teaching and the experience that children should have in school classrooms are not only matters for empirical research: important questions of value are involved. Nevertheless, a decade on from the Three Wise Men's deliberations, the body of evidence on what actually happens in our primary classrooms, on the nature and extent of changes that have taken place and on the effects of different teaching approaches, has grown considerably. This places us in a better position to consider some of these important questions about primary teaching, informed not only by aspirations and beliefs, but also by evidence of what actually happens in classrooms (Hastings 1998).

Group seating and its rationale

In many western countries, a man ties a long piece of material around his neck when he needs to look smart. If he does otherwise, others notice and, generally privately, entertain uncomplimentary explanations for this aberrant behaviour. We rarely ask why tie wearing is expected, it just is. Indeed, it is rare that we reflect on the rationale for many standard and accepted practices – unless prompted.

Organizing primary classrooms so that children sit in groups is standard practice. We hardly seem to need evidence to substantiate this everyday observation, but plenty exists (Bealing 1972; Galton *et al.* 1980; Bennett *et al.* 1984; Mortimore *et al.* 1988; Tizard *et al.* 1988; Alexander 1991; Blatchford and Kutnick 1999; Galton *et al.* 1999; McPake *et al.* 1999; Gipps *et al.* 2000; Osborn *et al.* 2000). The period over which these studies were undertaken and the fact that the overwhelming majority, and in some cases all, of the classrooms observed were arranged with children sitting in groups, amply demonstrate the extent to which the practice has been standard, at least in England and Scotland. Precisely because it is such established practice, the profession rarely reflects on why classrooms are so commonly organized like this. However, when the question is posed, as we have done to groups of teachers on an informal basis, four reasons are generally offered:

• to support small-group teaching;
• to support collaboration in learning within groups of children;
• as part of a strategy of 'ability grouping' or setting within a class;
• to facilitate access to resources which, when placed in the centre of a group of children, can be reached by all.

In the following sections we consider each of these reasons in more depth, taking the case in principle and in practice, as informed by evidence from classrooms.

Group seating for small-group teaching

As we noted a few paragraphs ago, the strategy of teachers working with groups of children within a class was strongly endorsed by the Plowden committee as a mode of teaching. In the committee's view, small-group teaching was a valuable compromise between the merits of giving each child individual attention and the consequence that, in a normal class, each child's ration would amount to only a few minutes each day. By spending time with groups of children, brought together for a particular teaching purpose, the committee reasoned, teachers can adjust their teaching to the needs of the individuals within the group to a greater extent than when working with the whole class, while also ensuring that all children receive more direct contact with their teacher. Although the committee did not have access to the research which now starkly illustrates the inverse relationship between the time that a teacher devotes to one-to-one interactions and the teacher contact that the average child gets, the unavoidable consequences of a 1:30 teacher–pupil ratio were clear to its members.

If a teacher is to work with groups of children and to move between these groups, it makes sense that children should be seated together as groups and also apart from other groups, and even greater sense if the activity is to be interactive. Sitting around a surface allows every individual to have easy eye contact with every other and therefore supports attention to whoever is contributing at a particular moment, whether it is the teacher or a group member. In this context, there is an evident consistency between what the teacher is trying to do, what the pupils are to do, the kind of interaction that is intended and the configuration of the furniture. So, group seating seems to be a good idea for small-group teaching and, to the extent that primary teachers make use of small-group teaching, this would be a good way to organize classrooms.

The case in principle is clear, but we need to enquire about the extent to which small-group teaching actually takes place. Primary classrooms may be arranged to support small-group teaching, but how much small-group teaching happens in practice? To answer this question we need evidence gathered from within primary classrooms, which is both sound and extensive. Studies of classroom teaching using detailed observation are labour intensive and therefore expensive to undertake on any scale and, as a consequence, the number of such studies is limited. However, if we can pool the evidence from several studies, the quality of the picture that emerges is enriched. Croll (1996a), Galton, *et al.* (1999) and Pollard *et al.* (2000) have all recently drawn together research evidence in this way, while simultaneously pointing out that it has to be done with some caution, not only with respect to when and where evidence was gathered and to the samples involved, but also to how the data were collected. In particular, the definitions and use of categories within observation schedules may differ, even when similar labels are used. This means that data from superficially similar studies may not always permit direct comparison, let alone collation.

Bearing these cautionary notes in mind, it is possible to view together evidence from a number of studies, undertaken in both Key Stage 1 (formerly 'Infant') and Key Stage 2 (formerly 'Junior') classrooms from the mid-1970s, as most employed very similar observation systems. Prominent among these are studies conducted by Maurice Galton, then at the University of Leicester, and his colleagues. We can also draw on evidence from the Primary Assessment, Curriculum and Experience (PACE) project, which followed a cohort of children through from their first days in Year 1 to their graduation from primary education at the end of Year 6 in 1996. In each of the study's six years, observations were completed of the same 54 children, 6 in each of nine schools, and their teachers. PACE has been reported in four books to date (Pollard *et al.* 1994; Croll 1996b; Osborn *et al.* 2000; Pollard *et al.* 2000).

Table 1.1 presents the data from seven major observational studies, including the Observational Research and Classroom Learning Evaluation (ORACLE) and PACE projects, which have recorded teachers' interactions with individuals, groups and the whole class. The figures are percentages of teachers' interactions, not percentages of their time in the classroom, although, in practice, the two sets would not now differ too much as recent studies have found that teachers spend upwards of 90 per cent of their time in the classroom engaged with children in one way or another. Back in the 1970s, it was about 80 per cent (Galton *et al.* 1980) but over the intervening years primary teaching has become an even busier business.

The studies listed in Table 1.1 span a period of unprecedented policy-led changes in primary education, yet, while the data suggest that changes have been taking place in primary teaching, they also demonstrate consistency. Teachers' interactions with individuals, groups and the whole class seem to have changed although in every study teachers engaged more with individuals than with the whole class, and more with the whole class than with groups. However, the reason for introducing the evidence

Table 1.1 Summary of observational studies of distribution of English primary teachers' interactions with pupils by context as percentages of all teacher–pupil interactions

| Project details | Key stage | Data collection | % of observed teacher interactions with pupils | | |
			1–1	Group	Class
ORACLE (Galton et al. 1980)		Late 1970s			
58 classes	2		72	9	19
40 classes	2		69	15	16
One in Five (Croll and Moses 1985)		Early 1980s			
32 classes	2		51	18	30
PRISMS (Galton and Patrick 1990)	1	Early 1980s	61	13	26
	2		58	16	26
School Matters (Mortimore et al. 1988)					
Year 4 classes in 50 schools	2	Mid-1980s	67	9	23
Year 5 classes in 50 schools	2		63	11	24
INCSS (Galton et al. 1988)	2	1989/90	59	18	23
PACE (Osborn 2001, personal communication)					
Year 1 9 classes	1	1990/1	45	22	33
Year 2 9 classes	1	1991/2	49	17	34
Year 3 9 classes	2	1992/3	57	14	29
Year 4 9 classes	2	1993/4	55	13	32
Year 5 9 classes	2	1994/5	57	16	28
Year 6 9 classes	2	1995/6	44	17	39
ORACLE 2 (Galton et al. 1999)					
28 classes	2	1996	48	16	35

Note: The PACE figures have not been published in this form by the PACE team but have been developed from information kindly provided by Marilyn Osborn.

in Table 1.1 at this stage is our interest in the use that is made of small-group teaching. The essence of small-group teaching is teachers working and interacting with groups, rather than individuals or the whole class. Thus the more that small-group teaching is used, the greater will be the proportion of interactions teachers have with groups. A glance down the 'Group' column in Table1.1 reveals that groups have consistently accounted for just 9–22 per cent of teachers' interactions with pupils – always less than class and one-to-one interactions.

These figures suggest that the Plowden committee's enthusiasm for small-group teaching has not been shared in teachers' practice over the last 30 years or so. Indeed, depending on how teaching is defined, these figures could give an inflated impression of the use of small-group teaching, as not all teachers' interactions with groups will be work-related. As well as having conversations with children about the curriculum and their work, teachers manage matters of routine (such as distribution of resources), deal with disputes and disruption and engage in small talk. So, for example, when a teacher goes to a group of children sitting together to have a word about arrangements for the afternoon's PE session, this would be recorded as interaction with a group, but might not be considered by all as 'teaching'. If *all* interactions are understood to be part of 'teaching', as well as being part of a teacher's job, then the recorded split between individual, group and class interactions reflects use of these three teaching approaches. However, if we think of 'teaching' as including only those interactions that are explicitly curriculum related, we have to ask about their frequency within individual, group and whole-class interactions as recorded in these studies. The ORACLE projects provide the clearest evidence.

The 1996 ORACLE 2 observations found that 'task' (i.e. curriculum-related) interactions accounted for 21 per cent of one-to-one, 36 per cent of group and 49 per cent of whole-class interactions (Galton *et al.* 1999). As interactions with groups accounted for just 16 per cent of teachers' communications with pupils and only 36 per cent of these were curriculum related, we can infer that small-group teaching has been rather infrequently used in most classrooms. Teaching small groups may be a valuable strategy, but these studies suggest that there has not been much of it about!

This inference from observations of teachers is strengthened by evidence from analyses of how pupils spend their time. In a recent study of Scottish primary classrooms, children were with their teacher as a member a group for just 6–9 per cent of their classroom time (McPake *et al*. 1999). Meanwhile, both ORACLE 2 and PACE found that Key Stage 2 pupils in English classrooms spent less than 4 per cent of their time in groups with their teachers. The figure was higher, around 6 to 10 per cent, for the PACE cohort when they were in Key Stage 1.

The PACE project even offers a third view on the prevalence of small-group teaching. As well as recording pupils' interactions and teachers' communication with children, the observers noted the 'main pedagogic context' of a teacher's activities at the end of each six-minute observation period. Where there was more than one context, a mix of two could be noted. The Key Stage 1 teachers used 'group work' as their main teaching method in a quarter of observations, whole-class and individual work each for about a third, and a mix of methods for the remaining sessions. However, as the children moved through Key Stage 2, working with a group declined in use as a teaching strategy and was the main method in only around 10 per cent of observation sessions each year. In contrast, a marked increase in the use of individual work was evident (Osborn *et al*. 2000).

The picture from research evidence is clear and consistent, although possibly surprising. Primary teachers in the UK interact with children in groups a good deal less than as whole classes or as individuals. This is true in both key stages. Although teachers are more inclined to work with groups with younger children, it is clear that small-group teaching has not been a common feature of classroom practice or of children's experience. Implementation of the NLS and NNS may well have modified this picture. Indeed, the limited evidence available so far suggests that, as might be predicted, teachers are giving more time to whole-class and group interactions and less attention to individuals (Alexander 2000). However, even with this shift, small-group teaching remains the least used of the three contexts in which teachers engage with children, as it has been since systematic studies of classroom interactions began in the early 1970s.

Returning with this conclusion to the issue of group seating and its rationale, we seem to have a situation in which primary classrooms across the country are organized partly to facilitate a method of teaching that is little used, especially in Key Stage 2. The argument for children sitting in a group to be taught as a group is simple and if group teaching was extensively used, the case for having classrooms organized this way would be strong, but it is not. Children sit in groups but are rarely taught as groups, so group teaching is not, on its own, a good reason to have group seating as the standard arrangement for primary classrooms.

Group seating for collaborative learning

A second and powerful argument for group seating is that it encourages collaboration and supports the interactions and discussions through which learning happens. The case for collaboration in learning, drawn from theory and from research, is strong and generally accepted – at least in principle – among primary educators. If children are to work together, their working environment needs to support collaboration and a group layout, in which a number of children sit around one working surface, fits the bill.

As with small-group teaching, the essence of the argument in favour of group seating for collaborative learning is that the physical context should support the teaching and learning method. When children are to work together, their workspace needs to allow eye contact, discussion, sight and use of shared materials and resources: it needs to support collaboration. The argument here is also clear and persuasive. We know that children do sit in groups and we know that the intention to stimulate and support learning through collaborative activities is a good reason to arrange classrooms this way. But are these intentions realized in practice? In other words how much collaboration in learning is planned or happening in our primary classrooms?

Before examining the evidence, some clarification is necessary. First, we need to recognize that collaboration in learning does not have to involve a group. It can happen in pairs as well as in groups of three or more. Indeed, there is a mountain of literature and plenty of evidence on the power of pairs working together, in peer tutoring or other peer-assisted learning relationships (e.g.

Topping and Ehly 1998). Second, children can sometimes collaborate over an activity for which their teacher has neither planned nor sought collaboration – as, for example, when two children each have the same individual work to do but make sense of it together. Of course, just as collaboration can happen when it is not intended, the reverse can also arise, as when some children opt out and, in effect, suspend their group membership – passively or actively. These points are important because they alert us to the fact that, if collaboration is examined only through records of children's interactions with one another, or only through an analysis of what teachers intend in the activities they set, the inferences drawn could be misleading. Both need to be considered, but we will begin with research on children's interactions with one another where, once more, differences between the observation systems used in different studies mean that the results are best used to construct a general picture rather than for fine-grained analyses and comparisons.

Children in primary classrooms in England now spend more of their time in conversation with other children than they used to. Back in 1976, the average pupil was interacting with at least one other child in 19 per cent of observations, but in 1996 this had risen to 27 per cent (Galton *et al.* 1999). This could mean that classrooms have become more disorderly, with children spending more time chatting, but it does not. The ORACLE observation system codes the focus of interactions, as well as their frequency, and the resulting data reveals that the balance between 'work' and 'non-work' interactions among pupils has shifted from a little over 1:2 in 1976 to 1:1 in 1996. In fact, the whole increase in pupil–pupil interactions over the 20-year period between the two ORACLE studies was work related: the amount of social chat had not changed (Galton *et al.* 1999). However, even with this increase, ORACLE 2 pupils were only recorded as actively working with at least one other in 13.5 per cent of observations.

The PACE team also gathered evidence on collaboration by sampling its 54 target children's interactions in each of their six years in primary education. Consistent with other studies' findings, across its six years, PACE project pupils spent their time largely alone, interacting with nobody – in this case for an average of 40 per cent of observations. Like their ORACLE 2 peers, they communicated with peers for around a quarter of their classroom time and mostly with just one other child. In fact, interactions with just one peer were twice as common as those with two or more, which accounted for an average of just 8 per cent of children's time (Osborn *et al.* 2000). Work related or not, conversations among groups of children were therefore rare.

McPake and her colleagues' observations in Scottish primary classrooms distinguished interactions by the nature of the task pupils were engaged in, as intended by the teacher. When observing a child interacting during a 'joint task of pair or small group which requires positive collaboration towards a joint outcome', the observation was coded as 'collaborative work', but if the task was individual and did not entail collaboration it would be coded as 'social interaction' – whether or not the interaction was work related or just chat (McPake, *et al.* 1999: 59). Defined this way, 'collaborative work' accounted for a consistent 5 to 6 per cent of pupils' observed time. However, as collaborative tasks and collaborative working do not necessarily require continuous interaction, this is not a direct measure of either work-related interactions or of the amount of collaborative work set. The figures do, however, suggest that collaborative tasks, involving two or more children, were not prominent in these classrooms.

More direct information about the use of collaborative learning comes from records of the activities that children are set. The first ORACLE project of Key Stage 2 classes (Galton *et al.* 1980) and a study of Key Stage 1 classes in London (Tizard *et al.* 1988) both found that, despite the fact that children sat in groups, individual work was predominant. For Tizard's infants, group work was noted in 3 to 7 per cent of observations across three years, while their older contemporaries worked alone for 68 per cent of the time in the London Junior School Project classrooms where 'not a great deal of collaborative work was observed' (Mortimore *et al.* 1988: 82) – words that could equally have been written at the conclusion of Alexander's (1991) investigation of primary education in Leeds. In small primary schools, children were observed working in paired or group activities for 9 per cent of their time – and individually for over 80 per cent (Hargreaves 1990). However, by 1996, and using the same observation schedule, ORACLE 2 observers were noting more than double this frequency in a different sample of primary schools.

This indication of a marked increase in the use of collaborative learning tasks was not evident in the PACE data, however. As with the observations of teachers, the 'pedagogic context' was noted at the end of each PACE child observation session. In 1991 and 1992, when the PACE children were in Year 1 and Year 2, 'group work' was recorded in just under 20 per cent of observations, but in each of their four years in Key Stage 2 the figure was below 10 per cent, although some of the time coded as a mix of activities will have included some collaborative work.

To summarize, although there are indications that work-related interactions between children have increased, they account for less than 15 per cent of pupils' time. This collaboration takes place mostly between pairs. Collaboration within a group is rare in most classrooms, as are tasks in which teachers specifically intend children to collaborate. There are indications that practice varies a good deal between classrooms and also that collaborative work is more commonly used in Key Stage 1.

The evidence reviewed here will paint a disappointing picture for any to whom it is unfamiliar, especially if they are committed to the use and development of collaboration in learning. The theoretical case for using collaborative learning activities is strong and there is a good deal of evidence from intervention studies, especially from North America, of the benefits of carefully planned and well structured activities requiring collaboration. For a good variety of reasons, well considered by others (e.g. Galton and Williamson 1992; Kutnick and Manson 2000), however, the evidence continues to be that teachers in UK primary schools make little use of collaborative learning activities. This leaves us in a position where there is a persuasive and rational case for using group seating to support collaboration but where there is also consistent evidence showing that we have one but not much of the other. Children *sit* in groups but are infrequently asked to *work* as groups: most of their work is individual or whole-class activity.

Group seating for 'ability grouping'

A third reason proffered for using group seating is that it facilitates 'ability grouping'. This is an interesting but different type of reason from the two already considered in that it has less direct relationships with teaching methods and intended interactions.

Decisions about who sits where in a classroom are generally based on a number of considerations. Some teachers plan for all seating groups to be mixed in attainment or gender while others seek homogeneity and have children sitting in single-sex groups or at tables differentiated by attainment. Still others allow children's friendships to inform the arrangements, often giving rise to single-sex groups, while just about every teacher will also make adjustments to seating arrangements if behaviour becomes an issue (Alexander 1992; Wragg 1993; Blatchford and Kutnick 1999; Osborn *et al.* 2000). Seating groups are not necessarily the same as, or necessary for, 'ability groups'.

Planning and managing differentiated learning activities so that each child has activities appropriate to their current understanding, skill and confidence, has long been an uncontroversial aspect of commended practice. It is generally achieved by allocating children to one of a limited number of 'groups', and often on the basis of attainment. There is no established term within primary education for this policy and practice. 'Ability grouping' is commonly used but is not satisfactory because 'ability' is so frequently understood as a fixed capacity, with the result that ability groups quickly come to be seen as 'intelligence groups', ranging from the bright to the irredeemably dim. 'Setting', the term used in secondary school contexts, now features in primary discourse when children are grouped for particular curriculum subjects and, less commonly, 'streaming' for groupings that remain unchanged across most or all subject areas.

Recent evidence from English primary schools indicates that, in one form or another, grouping children on the basis of attainment, usually through setting, is common (Ofsted 1998; Hallam *et al.* 1999). Schools differ a good deal in the way and the extent to which they set. Some set only within classes, others within year groups and still others between year groups. Similarly, there is variation in the extent to which setting is used across the different curriculum areas. These variations in practice are generally assumed to reflect differences in philosophy, but recent evidence suggests that grouping practices do not have a clear relationship to aims, at either the class or whole-school levels (Blatchford and Kutnick 1999; Hallam and Ireson 2001). Hallam and Ireson report that schools in their sample tended to have very similar educational aims. However, they differed a good deal in the grouping practices that they used and believed in, yet each school believed that its own chosen approach to grouping was effective in improving the same educational outcomes.

These two forms of grouping, physically in the configuration of seating arrangements and pedagogically through differentiation of learning activities, may produce coincident allocations: children in the same set may also sit together. But this is not a necessary outcome. Indeed, in many classrooms seating arrangements are deliberately planned so that children from *different* sets sit together at each table in 'mixed ability' groups. For some activities, children within these seating groups will each work on a task allocated for their set: for other activities they may all move to different tables or spaces. When seating groups do not correspond to setting arrangements, the organization of life within a classroom or school can seem completely bewildering to a visitor. However, the outsider will generally also be struck by the fact that everyone seems to know what they are doing. A randomly identified child understands well that she is in the 'Galapagos Islands' for literacy and in the 'Arctic Foxes' for numeracy, while her base is 'Blue Group' where she works along with friends from other literacy and numeracy sets. In some classrooms, however, teachers arrange seating to reflect sets which, if they do not differ between curriculum subjects, effectively become streamed groups, differentiated on the basis of the teacher's assessment of general attainment or potential.

There is, therefore, only a limited sense in which 'ability grouping' or setting is an argument for sitting children in groups in primary classrooms. Sets and seating groups do not have to have the same membership, and frequently do not. Moreover, a set brought together for a learning purpose need not sit in a group configuration. The fact that they constitute a 'set group' does not necessitate them sitting as a group – unless, of course, they are to work together in collaboration or are to work directly with their teacher as a group, in which case the argument for the group seating is that it facilitates collaboration or small-group teaching, not 'ability grouping'.

Group seating for access to resources

The fourth commonly suggested benefit of routinely seating children in groups is that the arrangement allows six or eight children each to reach and use one centrally placed set of resources, such as pens, colours, glue, etc. This is self-evidently true. If children were to be seated in separate pairs or a horseshoe, for instance, resource sets would either have to increase in number or be passed more frequently between children. We have no challenge to this argument for group seating: it reflects some practical realities. However, its strength as a justification for group seating as a standard arrangement for classrooms is less certain.

Matching classroom organization and learning

We have considered four frequently offered reasons for arranging primary classrooms so that children sit in groups. The first two, that group seating supports small-group teaching and collaboration within groups, are sound in principle. In each case the argument is that the seating arrangement should reflect and support the use of a particular teaching or learning strategy. The problem is not in the logic of this case but in the fact that evidence from primary classrooms shows that neither of these two pedagogic practices is actually used very often. The case for children sitting around tables in order to be taught together or to work together as a group only makes sense if group teaching and group work are commonly used teaching methods – but they are not. If they were, the merits of group seating would be increasingly evident.

The third argument, that group seating supports 'ability grouping' is, in our view, simply a confused case. It arises from a failure to distinguish between the notion of a group as a category and a group as a spatial configuration. The two types of group have no necessary relationship. The final argument, that group seating enables a number of children all to reach a single set of resources is, as we have just suggested, valid but hardly a strong case on its own. Yet, of the four arguments considered, it seems to be the only one that is both logically coherent *and* reflects what actually happens in primary classrooms.

If it is sensible for classroom organization to match and support children's learning – a case to which we wholly subscribe – we need to consider how, day by day, children are asked to learn. Teaching methods have not followed group seating arrangements, and nor should they have done. It is teaching methods that should determine classroom organization, not *vice versa*.

The evidence presented in Table 1.1 showed that teachers are almost frenetically busy interacting with children. Observations of children also produce a consistent picture but it is a very different one. Teachers are busy interacting with children, but children are not busy interacting with their teachers. With one teacher and around 30 children, each child has only limited teacher contact. In fact, the 'typical primary child' spends most of their classroom time working alone or with other children and gets most of their direct teacher contact as a member of the whole class, not as an individual (Galton *et al.* 1980; Alexander 1992; Galton *et al.* 1999; Pollard *et al.* 2000). This well-established observation is important; so important that it bears repetition. Children in English primary classes spend most of their time in the classroom *without* their teacher. By way of illustration, ORACLE 2 recorded children as *not* engaged with their teacher in more than 70 per cent of observations (Galton *et al.* 1999). Direct teacher contact is certainly important in children's learning but the stark and persistent reality of everyday classrooms has been that children work without their teacher for most of the time. Moreover, most of their contact with their teacher happens when the teacher is working with the whole class. Consequently, in classes where teachers do more whole-class activity, children get more direct teacher contact. The recent small-scale study by McPake *et al.* (1999) of 12 Scottish primary classrooms illustrates this well. Overall, pupils were in direct contact with their teacher for 41 per cent of their classroom time. This was achieved because, for 32 per cent of the time, their teacher was interacting with the whole class. In contrast with the children in English primary schools in the ORACLE and PACE studies, the pupils in McPake's classes in Scotland spent as much time with their teacher as without them, although there was substantial variation between classes and between year groups. In schools in countries where whole-class teaching and children demonstrating or explaining to the whole class are popular teaching strategies, pupils spend much less time working independently of their teacher (Alexander 2000).

In pondering how classrooms might be organized better, we need to think not only about what teachers do but also about what children are doing, and are meant to be doing, when they are not with their teacher. Broadly, teachers expect children to be busy with one of two types of activity – working alone or working in collaboration with one or more peers, most often the first. PACE, for example, recorded individual work for more than 50 per cent of all pupils' activities in Key Stage 2 classes (Pollard *et al.* 2000). The asymmetrical relationship between group seating and the individual work that children are given is highlighted by two studies that recorded pupils' seating context ('base') and the nature of their work activity ('team') simultaneously. In small schools, children's base was pairs or groups in 70 per cent of observations, yet their work was individual in 80 per cent of observations (Hargreaves 1990). In ORACLE 2 classrooms, two-thirds of observations recorded children sitting in groups and about the same proportion noted them as working alone. This mismatch between working context and task is stark and enduring for, even though teachers now spend more time working with their classes as a whole, individual work remains the most common type of task for children when they are not with their teacher.

Through all the changes that have taken place in English primary schools over the last two or three decades, group seating has remained as the standard way of organizing a classroom. In fact, practice has been so consistent that Galton and his colleagues were able to use precisely the same words to report on their findings in 1999 as they had 20 years earlier when they described children as mainly 'seated in groups around flat topped tables or desks drawn together to form working surfaces' (Galton *et al.* 1999: 41) (see also Galton *et al.* 1980: 59). Throughout this time, the mismatch we have discussed has been evident. The case for reviewing the standard practice of group seating and for reconsidering what makes for 'good practice' in classroom organization is now strong.

2 Does classroom organization matter?

The evidence reviewed in Chapter 1 begs the question as to why primary classrooms are still generally arranged in grouped tables, despite the fact that groups would appear to be ill-suited to supporting the two activities that account for most of children's classroom time – engaging with their teacher in whole-class sessions and working alone. According to Alexander (1992: 68) the explanation lies in the fact that 'the physical arrangement of grouping in primary schools has acquired such a powerful doctrinal status that no other arrangement is even entertained'. His case was that grouping, most explicitly represented in the arrangement of the classroom environment, had become so integral to the culture and language of primary education that its functions and operation were at best taken for granted and at worst resulted in questions about the functions of grouping being regarded as 'an impertinence'. The Three Wise Men, of whom Alexander was one, risked the charge of 'impertinence' by raising the matter again in their influential discussion document where they focused on the purposes of grouping: 'All too often there may be a mismatch between the collaborative setting of the group and the individual learning tasks which are given to pupils. The result is that the setting may distract pupils from their work' (Alexander *et al.* 1992, para. 96.)

A 'mismatch' of task and setting can be rectified in several ways – by changing tasks to match settings, settings to match tasks or possibly both to produce alignment. There are certainly strong arguments for increasing the use of cooperative group work, supported by a growing body of evidence of its effectiveness. As we noted in Chapter 1, there are also indications that recent developments in the teaching of literacy and mathematics in England have increased the use of small-group teaching. To the extent that either of these teaching strategies increases in use, so the appropriateness of group seating will increase. Alternatively, or additionally, a case could be made for changing the physical and social setting to match the teaching strategies that teachers use most frequently. Indeed, following publication of the Three Wise Men's report, McNamara and Waugh (1993) argued for a 'horseshoe' as the best arrangement of furniture for the mix of teaching and learning activities found in most primary classrooms. However, they were unable to offer more than anecdotal evidence of its benefits. Horseshoe layouts may well have merit but in the absence of evidence there is an obvious danger of the profession replacing one mode of organization – initially established by argument, possibly driven by dogma and now maintained by custom and habit – with another which is no better supported by evidence of its consequences.

So, before contemplating, let alone urging, changes in practice that would result in a better match between task and setting, we need to ask and answer some clear factual questions about the differences that seating arrangements actually make to teaching and learning. There are three that will concern us in this chapter:

- Do seating arrangements actually make any difference to teaching and learning? The argument for matching tasks and settings may have common-sense appeal, but does matching really make any difference?
- If seating arrangements do make a difference, is that difference educationally important?
- If seating arrangements matter, do they matter for *all* pupils?

Before delving into sources where we might find evidence relevant to these questions, a few points about research methods need to be considered.

First, it will be evident that any investigation of whether seating arrangements make a difference will have to compare the effects of children working in classrooms organized in at least two settings. Second, for the conclusions to be robust, any study will have to ensure that seating arrangements are the *only* difference in children's experience of working in the two contexts. This degree of control could be achieved by creating entirely artificial 'laboratory' classroom environments into which children are invited solely for the purpose of the research. However, confidence in generalizing findings from this entirely artificial context to real classrooms would be limited. Alternatively, the research could be undertaken in live school settings. 'Real world' research increases confidence in generalizing the findings to other real settings. However, it faces difficulties in ensuring that it is only the factor under investigation that is responsible for any differences in outcome. Keeping other factors constant or under control is much more difficult in a real school environment than in artificial 'laboratory' contexts.

A partial solution to the problems of comparing groups of children working in different seating arrangements and also in different classrooms with their own teachers, is to compare the outcomes of the *same* classes and teachers working under different conditions. In this type of research, the same children, in the same classroom and with the same teacher are studied while working in two or more seating arrangements. In practice, it is exactly this style of quasi-experimental research that has been most commonly used in investigations of the effects of different classroom configurations. Typically, classes have been studied as they worked on a given type of task, usually individual work, in one arrangement for a period, then in another for a similar period and then reverted to first. These periods have typically been short – just a matter of a week or two in most cases.

The third point we need to note about research methods before examining the evidence has to do with the outcomes that are to be monitored. The most important question to be asked about any educational practice is whether it benefits children's education more than other possible practices. In asking this question about classroom organization, the potential educationally important outcomes that classroom layout might affect have to be identified and defined in such a way that they can be assessed. Educational outcomes that are generally agreed as being important include not only progress and attainment in the curriculum, but also curiosity, confidence and enjoyment of learning. Classroom processes are also important outcomes in their own right, including behaviour and the extent to which children actively engage with their work and are not passively or actively distracted from it. But of all the educational outcomes, attainment is arguably the most significant. If classroom organization has an impact on children's learning and attainment, with some classroom arrangements leading to greater academic progress than others, teachers ought to know about it. But to date, only one study has been published in which the impact of seating on attainment was assessed (Bennett and Blundell 1983). The study was undertaken, well before the introduction of the National Curriculum, in a school selected for its exceptionally tightly structured curriculum which allowed for comparison of both the quantity and quality of individual work completed in reading, maths and language when children worked seated in groups and in rows. The findings were less than completely clear. More work was completed when children sat in rows but no significant differences in quality emerged. However, the periods of working in groups and in rows were acknowledged as short, just two weeks, and may well have been too limited for differences in rates of progress to become evident.

If the organization of classrooms affects learning, it is likely to be because it influences how teachers teach and interact with children, how children work and their attention to learning activities. There is, therefore, a good case to be made for examining whether different seating arrangements give rise to important differences in classroom processes and, in particular, to children's attention. Children's attention, defined as 'time on-task' or 'task engagement time', has been a common focus of attention in research assessing the impact of classroom seating. Of course, 'time on-task' is not a measure of learning but of the extent to which children's attention is focused on the work they are meant to be doing. Its use as an indicator presupposes that learning requires attention to be focused on relevant activities: 'Time is a necessary, but not sufficient, condition for learning. Learning takes time, but providing time does not in itself ensure that learning will take place' was how Karweit (1984: 33) expressed it. Without attention, learning cannot happen: with attention, it may do.

The final points to be made about aspects of research methods have to do with the types of classroom arrangement that have been investigated, and with the task context. Nearly all published studies have compared the effects of just two seating arrangements on children's time on-task when working on an individual activity. These have been groups, as generally found in UK primary classrooms, and 'rows'. We have placed rows between quotation marks because the term needs to be handled with caution. In this context, rows does not mean parallel lines of adjoining tables with pupils all facing the front of a classroom, although it could mean this. The two conditions which all rows arrangements have fulfilled have been that no pupil sits with another facing them across the same surface and that there is somewhere in the room where the teacher can stand and readily have eye contact with every child, without any having to turn around more than 90 degrees. In practice, most studies have tried layouts in which children sit in pairs at tables and, broadly speaking, face in the same direction. For shorthand, however, all of these arrangements are called rows. Armed with these understandings, we can now turn to consider what published research has to offer that is relevant to answering the three questions identified before this brief but necessary detour into matters of research design.

Do seating arrangements actually make any difference to teaching and learning?

It is not only recently that classroom seating has attracted research interest. Wheldall and Glynn (1989) and Merrett (1994) refer to isolated studies from the 1920s and 1930s, but the main body of evidence begins in 1979 with the publication of a study in the USA (Axelrod *et al.* 1979) which examined the on-task and disruptive behaviour rates of a class of 7- and 8-year-olds when seated in groups and in rows. The finding was that average on-task levels were markedly higher and rates of disruption were substantially lower when the class sat in rows rather than around tables in groups. There were, of course, day to day variations as children's attention is affected by plenty of factors other than how they are sitting, but there was no doubt that the children worked and behaved differently in the two contexts.

The first British study was a partial replication of Axelrod's work and involved two parallel classes of 10- and 11-year-olds and their teachers (Wheldall *et al.* 1981). For the first two weeks, the proportion of time that children spent working on individual tasks while sitting in their usual groups was recorded. For the next two weeks, the classes sat in rows and, for a final two-week phase they moved back to their usual group seating. As in the American study, in both classes the data revealed clear differences between the average time on-task in the two settings. Children spent more time involved with their individual tasks in the rows phase than when they worked in groups.

Table 2.1, adapted from one previously published elsewhere (Hastings *et al.* 1996), draws together the data from Wheldall and a number of similar studies completed by or with teachers in English schools. As well as giving brief details of the classes involved in each study, the table shows the average time on-task recorded in each phase of working in groups and in rows. The number of figures in the groups and rows columns for each study reflects the number of phases in its design. So, for example, in the second study by Kevin Wheldall (Wheldall and Lam 1987), pupils were monitored over four phases, two when they worked in groups and two in rows.

A glance down the two columns of Table 2.1 showing percentage time on-task when children sat in groups and in rows reveals that, without exception, the figures are higher for rows than for groups in every class in every study. Although each of these studies is small and incapable of sustaining more general conclusions on its own, the consistency of the findings across the studies, undertaken at different times, in different types of school and in different places, does provide a basis for the general conclusion that children find it easier to focus on their individual tasks when sitting in the less social context provided by rows than when grouped at a table with several peers. However, before accepting this case as proven, it is important to ask whether there is any other plausible explanation for this consistent pattern of results. In this case, there is another possibility: it could be that it is change itself that has produced the effect. The

Table 2.1 Summary of the design and results of studies of class average time on-task (%) seated in groups and 'rows' for individual tasks

Details of research	% time on-task in groups	% time on-task in rows	(Average) % increase in time on-task for rows over groups
Wheldall et al. (1981): 2 mainstream classes; 2 weeks in each phase	72, 73	85	20
Class 1: 28 10/11-year-olds Class 2: 25 10/11-year-olds	68, 73	92	30
Wheldall and Lam (1987): 3 special school (EBD) classes; 4, 3, 3 and 3 week phases	29, 33	72, 67	124
Class 1: 14/15-year-olds	34, 39	74, 71	99
Class 2: 13/14-year-olds Class 3: 12/13-year-olds	38, 36	73, 70	93
Yeomans (1989): 2 weeks in each phase Mainstream class of 8/9-year-olds	49, 38	79	82
Hastings and Schwieso (1995): (A) 2 mainstream classes; 2 weeks in each phase			
Class 1: 31 9/11-year-olds	56	75, 79	37
Class 2: 31 9/11-year-olds	66, 65	76	16
(B) 3 weeks in each phase Mainstream class of 7/8-year-olds	48	78	63

Note: EBD = emotional and behavioural difficulties.
Source: Adapted from Hastings et al. (1996).

increased time on-task that each study found for rows might not be due to the seating arrangements but just to a 'change of scene'. If this was the explanation, a change to any other unfamiliar arrangements should have the same effect.

This possibility was checked in one of the studies listed in Table 2.1 (Hastings and Schwieso 1995) which examined the effect of moves to rows and groups for two classes whose normal seating was neither rows nor groups, but a kind of maze arrangement. The two classes tried the two unfamiliar arrangements of rows and groups in a different sequence. If change alone was responsible for increasing attention to task, both classes should produce the same pattern of results even though the new settings they were trying were different. This was not what happened. The outcome for both was that on-task levels were higher in rows than groups, irrespective of the order in which they tried them, indicating that the effect, in this and other studies listed in Table 2.1, is attributable to properties of the seating arrangements themselves and not to their novelty.

All of the studies in Table 2.1 assessed the effect on time on-task for individual work of a change from pupils' familiar group seating to rows. Before concluding this section, we should note a project with a different focus. Back in 1985, Rosenfeld *et al.* investigated the consequences of rows, circles and group seating arrangements for time on-task for children in some Californian elementary schools. In apparent contrast to all of the studies listed in Table 2.1, this study found that children generally spent more time on-task when seated in circles than in groups, with rows producing the *lowest* on-task rates of all three settings. The explanation for this pattern of findings? The task was brainstorming ideas for writing assignments, not completing individual work. Once this is known, it hardly seems surprising that children were more active in discussions when they sat in a class circle or in groups than when they sat in rows. After all, who would ever arrange a room in rows to hold a discussion? And yet, the finding that children are better able to concentrate on individual assignments when they are not asked to work at a table with a group of peers can still elicit surprise.

So, returning to the question at the head of this section, the research evidence is clear, and also entirely consistent with everyday expectations, and justifies an unqualified answer: 'Yes:

seating arrangements do make a difference to teaching and learning.'

If seating arrangements do make a difference, is that difference educationally important?

Finding that seating arrangements affect teaching and learning processes may not matter if the degree of difference made is not educationally significant. To decide whether the difference is important in educational terms we need to examine the nature and size of that difference.

The final column in Table 2.1 gives the difference between average on-task levels in the two conditions expressed as a percentage of the on-task rate in the group phase. For example, if a class moved from an average of 60 per cent on-task in groups to 90 per cent in rows, an increase of 30 percentage points, the figure in the final column would be 50 per cent. Examination of this final column shows that the actual increases range from a modest but worthwhile 16 per cent to an extraordinary 124 per cent. These are the extremes but, of the nine cases, all but two show increases of 30 per cent or more and in five cases the gain was more than 60 per cent. In just about any environment, improvements of 30, let alone 60 per cent or more, would warrant serious attention, especially when they are achieved at no cost!

Gains in the time that children spend actively engaged with their work, even though we are only considering individual work here, will not necessarily be directly reflected in learning and progress. On the other hand, it is barely conceivable that such large increases in working time will have no impact on learning and attainment, although there is currently no evidence available against which to test the proposition. But learning may benefit from these increases in time on-task in more indirect ways as well. More time on-task means less time is spent in distraction, fiddling with resources, social chat, watching the world go by or, much less frequently, actively disrupting others. The ORACLE 2 data reveals that the more distracted children receive the highest rates of one-to-one attention from their teachers, suggesting that much of this individual attention is teachers chivvying them back to work (Galton *et al.* 1999). If these children work more when seated in the less distracting context of rows, the need for teachers to refocus them onto their work reduces and, as a consequence, teachers will have more opportunities for curriculum-related interactions with the children, which should also benefit learning. Consistent with these possibilities, one of the studies we have already considered (Wheldall and Lam 1987) found rates of disruption to be three times lower in the rows seating phases: teachers also praised and commended children more.

To summarize, seating arrangements do seem to have educationally important effects on children's attention to individual work. However, the effects of seating arrangements do not seem to be limited to time on-task. When the match between task and setting is improved, a virtuous circle begins. Learning, behaviour and the tone of the classroom, reflected in teachers' use of praise and criticism, also benefit. Taken as a whole, the evidence indicates that the second question also warrants an affirmative answer: 'Seating arrangements do not just make a difference to the way children work, they make an educationally important difference.'

If seating arrangements matter, do they matter for *all* pupils?

The evidence supporting a 'yes' answer to the first two questions has been about class averages. The figures in Table 2.1, for example, are class *averages* for time on-task. As with all averages, there will be variation around the class average for time on-task, with some children being more distracted and less focused on their work than most, and others who manage to spend most, even all, of their time working. We have already reviewed the differences in class averages for time on-task in groups and rows, but two of the investigations listed in Table 2.1 examined how children differed in their responses to the two contexts (rows and groups) for individual work (Wheldall *et al.* 1981; Hastings and Schwieso 1995). Expressed more informally, these studies asked whether some children were more influenced by the seating arrangements than others and, if so, who was most and who least affected.

Both of these studies found exactly the same pattern in their data for individual children. Those who were most affected by the move to rows were those who were least on-task in the group arrangement. In other words, those who worked *least* when sitting in groups, gained *most* from the change to rows. Children who concentrated well on their individual tasks when sitting in groups were not much affected by the change to rows: they got on with their work however they sat. But the story was quite different for many of their classmates.

The figures from one of these studies makes the scale of the impact for these children clear. In one class of 32, the 8 children who were least on-task in groups, at just 38 per cent, moved to 72 per cent and 78 per cent in the two two-week periods in rows. In the parallel class, which spent two phases in groups, the figures for this 'low' group were 44 per cent and 46 per cent in groups and 72 per cent in rows (Hastings and Schwieso 1995). For some individuals, the effect was to treble their working time. In contrast, for the 8 children most able to focus when seated in groups, the change to rows made no appreciable difference. The inverse relationship between time on-task in groups and the improvement on moving to rows is important in its own right, but it also leads to differences in task involvement all but disappearing in the rows arrangement. When the classes were working in rows, the difference between the most and the least on-task pupils was small: when they worked in groups, the range was substantial.

The finding that it is the children who are least engaged with their individual work when sitting in groups who benefit most from a change to the less distracting setting of rows is also evident in the data for classes in Table 2.1. Across all of the studies, it is the classes with the lowest on-task levels in groups that gain most from the move to rows, as the figures in the final column emphasize. The data in the table also illustrate how this differential impact affects the variation between (in this case) classes, as the range of figures in the rows column is more limited than it is for groups.

Equipped with this evidence, we can move towards an answer to the third question. Every primary teacher has children in their class who seem to have considerably greater difficulty in concentrating than others. Often described as having 'short attention spans', these youngsters need directing back to their work with irritating frequency and seem to be distracted by everybody else's business. The evidence reviewed above suggests that these children may find it harder to concentrate than others but also demonstrates that the context in which they are routinely asked to complete individual work at least contributes to their problem: it may even *be* their problem. But is it such an unusual problem? After all, most teachers do not arrange for a group of friends to join them at the table when they have the task of preparing reports or a presentation for their school's governors. We even design our academic libraries with desks providing bays that shield us from the distracting, if fascinating, antics and quirks of other readers, and support attention to the task currently in hand.

So does classroom organization matter?

Existing evidence from research completed in real classrooms has provided a sound basis for venturing answers to each of the three questions posed at the start of this chapter:

- *Do seating arrangements actually make any difference to teaching and learning?* Yes. The mismatch between group seating and the individual work that children are asked to do when working without their teacher does matter. Seating arrangements make a difference.
- *If seating arrangements do make a difference, is that difference educationally important?* Yes. Classes spend a greater proportion of available time actively involved in individual work when working in rows rather than in groups. The difference is substantial. Behaviour also benefits.
- *If seating arrangements matter, do they matter for* all *pupils?* No. For some children seating arrangements seem to be of little or no significance; for most they matter and for a substantial minority they matter a great deal.

These answers are stated boldly, but there are boundaries to the fields in which they apply. First, all of the studies to which we have referred investigated just two seating arrangements – groups and some form of rows. Second, the effects of these two seating contexts have been monitored, in most cases, only for one aspect of classroom practice – work that teachers ask children to undertake on their own. Such individual work is common in UK primary classrooms but it is by no means the only kind of learning task arranged. While the evidence certainly shows that asking children to undertake individual work in the manifestly social context of a group makes life unnecessarily difficult for many, and exceptionally so for some, the implication of this evidence and of this discussion is not that rows should replace groups as the standard layout. This is, however, how some sections of the media have interpreted the evidence, but the real message makes less of a story for journalists. It is that the current practice of asking children to work alone while seated in groups warrants review, but this is a particular, well researched, instance of a more general and very simple principle: *Classrooms should be organized to match learning activities.*

The evidence reviewed in this and the previous chapter is not new. Indeed, some of it is certainly out of date in the sense that classroom practice has changed in subsequent years. As we have noted at several points, as we write, almost no evidence of how teachers and children interact and use their time has been gathered and published since implementation of the NLS and NNS, which have almost certainly increased teachers' use of whole-class and group teaching. While it is always better to have completely current evidence, in a fundamental respect its absence does not matter. It is for a principle and not for detailed recommendations for practice that the evidence so persuasively argues.

Matching learning contexts and activities: moving on

The evidence considered in these first two chapters highlights three important features of classroom life in English primary schools and, to varying degrees, in schools elsewhere. First, teachers plan for children to learn through five main types of activity. Children can be directly taught by their teachers – as individuals, in small groups and as a whole class – or, when not with their teacher, the requirement is usually that they should work alone or in collaboration. These five types of learning activity differ in many respects, including the numbers of people involved, the interactions that they entail and in the nature of the attention that they require. They also differ in the extent to which they are actually used in classrooms, with working alone and being taught as a member of the whole class tending to feature most prominently.

Second, most English primary classrooms are organized so that children sit in groups to work. Classrooms organized in other ways are not unknown but grouped seating is the norm across the sector.

Third, while group seating arrangements make sense for two of the five types of learning activity, they are not well suited to all and make learning through individual work demonstrably more difficult than it need be, and especially so for some young-sters. Children are often set the task of learning in a classroom organized in a manner that does not match and support the learning activity.

The research base for these three points is robust and highly relevant to the daily work of every primary schoolteacher and headteacher. It highlights aspects of practice as requiring recon-sideration and justifies a call for all schools and teachers to consider how they can secure a greater level of match between classroom seating arrangements and learning activities. Why this has not yet happened is a matter for speculation, but, in our view, there are a number of contributory factors. A good propor-tion of primary teachers and headteachers will not know of this research, but among those who are familiar with the evidence there is often caution about changing established practice. This reticence is not born of a philosophical or ideological commit-ment to group seating but reflects concern about the practical feasibility of reorganizing classrooms. A second concern, expressed by some, is whether others, especially colleagues, LEA staff, Ofsted inspectors and parents, would regard such an immediately vis-ible departure from normal practice as 'good practice'.

The first two chapters are offered as a contribution to the task of enabling primary teachers to become aware of the relevant research, but concerns about the feasibility of reorganizing class-rooms to support learning and about the likely reactions of others are best assuaged by accounts from the classrooms of teachers who have developed their practices along these lines. So we set out to find some of these pioneers.

Part 2
Daring to be different: tales from the frontier

3 Case studies

Bridging the gap between knowledge of research evidence and practice, as reflected in what people actually do, is always problematic. Many of us still take too little exercise even though we know, at least broadly, of research revealing the increased risks this brings. The same is true of smoking and alcohol consumption, of course. Information alone, it seems, is rarely sufficient for most of us to support a change in behaviour.

Organizing primary classrooms in groups is not a recognized addictive condition, but it is certainly a well established and resilient custom in schools across the UK, and now also in some other parts of the English-speaking world. Within the UK, any classroom in a state primary school that is not arranged in groups will generally attract curious, even suspicious, attention and the existence of research evidence showing that other classroom layouts might be better for some types of activity has not been sufficient to promote change. Although the teaching profession, a self-evidently well educated subsection of the population, has not developed its professional knowledge base and practices on the basis of research, there is increasing recognition that teaching should be informed by evidence of the effects of different practices and strategies. At present, however, the gap between the research evidence and the implementation of research-informed innovations is wide and remains in need of bridging. A valuable and possibly necessary component of any such bridge is a readily accessible set of examples, drawn from real classrooms, illustrating how practice can develop in ways that build on, or are consistent with, insights from robust research evidence. In the case of primary classroom organization, the need is for accounts of classrooms in which teachers work to ensure a good match between classroom seating and the demands of different types of learning activity.

The decision to undertake a small project to identify a sample of primary teachers who work in this way, to visit them and to learn about and then describe their practices and experiences was easy. Finding such teachers was not. Although we were looking for illustrative cases rather than a representative sample, we wanted examples from across the country. There is, of course, no list of such classrooms or teachers and, because inspection reports do not describe classroom practices at this level of detail, Ofsted's reports were of no assistance. It seemed likely, however, that those who visit schools would be well placed to have seen and noted examples of unusual practice. Educational psychologists and people working in a variety of capacities related to the education of children with special educational needs tend to visit plenty of classrooms, so we posted a brief account of the project and an invitation to contact us on two well-used electronic mailbases. Responses were interesting but limited. Many expressed interest in the project but did not know of any appropriate classrooms, but a few undertook to contact teachers who seemed to fit the bill to ask if they would take part. A minority returned with good news. Two educational psychologists reported that they worked in this way prior to recently qualifying and leaving classroom teaching, while some of their colleagues, also knowing the relevant research and generally prompted by observation of individual children whose behaviour and progress caused concern, said they frequently suggested that teachers should reconsider their classroom organization. A letter published in the *Times Educational Supplement* also yielded a few responses from teachers keen to have their classroom practices described.

Time and resources necessitated a rethink. We already knew of some of these innovative teachers through other professional activities but were able to extend the list with the names of a few others known to colleagues in LEAs. The final total was just 30 curious and willing, if slightly wary, participants from which to draw the cases planned for this book. In three instances – two in the Reading area and one in Nottinghamshire – more than one teacher in the school used classroom seating strategically, although the schools varied in the extent to which classroom organization is a matter of school policy. The others were all individual teachers of Key Stage 2 or, more unusually, Key Stage 1 classes who, for interestingly varied reasons, had come to arrange their classrooms other than in groups and, more importantly, to vary seating to match learning purposes.

We have no idea whether these 30 teachers represent a tiny or substantial proportion of all English primary teachers who work like this. The fact that some recently published books have made particular mention of individual cases of such teachers encountered in the course of research suggests that they remain rare and special. In his recent book reporting on observations in primary classrooms in five countries, Alexander (2000: 335) describes the practice of one teacher he observed in the USA:

> Alone of all the teachers we observed . . . this one Michigan teacher appeared to take the view that method and classroom layout should always align precisely with each other. If that meant moving the furniture several times a day, so be it. It was accomplished with remarkable speed and – even more remarkable when one considers the percussive impart of metal table legs on wooden floors – almost silently.

Similarly, Maurice Galton and his colleagues highlight the practice of one of their sample of English Key Stage 2 teachers whose children sit in a horseshoe formation that is changed when necessary to support other activities, including collaborative group work (Galton *et al.* 1999; Comber and Wall 2001). A third recent study found that all but 1 of 24 English teachers of Year 1 and Year 6 children, selected for their high levels of professional expertise, maintained the same classroom layout throughout the four school terms of the project: 'However, one particularly interesting teacher had introduced the norm of changing the layout to suit the type of lesson' (Gipps *et al.* 2000: 30).

The strategies used by these three teachers clearly struck the research teams (who encountered them by chance) as unusual, thoughtful and professionally very interesting. The classrooms of the 12 teachers whose approaches we describe in some detail in the following pages struck us similarly when we visited each in 1999/2000 to see how they operated. We observed in each classroom and held informal interviews with the teachers to learn how their current practice had developed; how it worked in detail; their perceptions of the costs and benefits of their approach; and of any reactions or comments they had noted from others. In some cases we also spoke with children and/or with the headteacher. Each of these accounts has been checked by the teacher for accuracy and is, with their and their school's agreement, published with the names of the teacher and school.

We are in no doubt that these teachers are exceptional, in every positive sense of the word. They work in very varied contexts and are by no means all experienced. Some teach in spacious classrooms while others work in cramped conditions. Some work in schools serving relatively affluent areas; others are in schools serving substantially disadvantaged communities. In every case, however, a strategy has been developed to suit local conditions as well as the principle of matching context to activity. The three schools in which more than one teacher works this way are presented first and followed by accounts of individual pioneers. All are offered to illustrate the ways in which the principle of matching classroom organization to learning activity can be realized in practice and to inspire and support confidence in others, hopefully including yourself, to review and develop their use of classroom organization to support learning more effectively.

A classroom organization website, currently under construction, is planned to provide a growing library of examples of practice in classroom organization and of teachers' accounts of their successes and disappointments in trying new approaches. It will also provide a forum for discussions about primary classroom organization, teaching and learning. It can be found at: http://education.ntu.ac.uk/research/primaryclassorg.

Geoffrey Field Junior School, Reading

Enter Geoffrey Field Junior School and you have no trouble determining where visitors should go. You are in the reception area with a soft seating corner to the right and the school's secretary facing and welcoming you. Four more desks in this large and bright foyer are for the headteacher, deputy-headteacher, the school's finance officer and a clerical assistant. The immediate impression is of a vibrant, well-organized and welcoming school.

The foyer-office works well in meeting the twin tasks of providing a relaxed and immediate welcome (especially for the many parents who do not readily approach school) and ensuring that no one enters without notice or permission. Having several people around in the reception area also serves a precautionary purpose for those fortunately rare but real occasions when a visitor arrives in an aggressive manner. Two rooms for confidential discussions, the school's 'Really Useful Room' and the 'Headteacher's Conference Room', are nearby.

Charlie Clare has been head of this large junior school in Reading for 11 years and leads a team of deputy-headteacher, 12 full-time teaching staff, five teaching facilitators, five learning support assistants (LSAs) supporting children with statements and a further two funded for additional literacy support. A committed office staff and caretaker complete the team.

The school is set in an estate to the south of the town centre with a high proportion of council-maintained housing. The crime rate is high and there is poverty. The estate stands in contrast to most of Reading – a prosperous Thames Valley metropolis where many new technology companies have established bases and where unemployment is so low that the recently opened stadium and new shopping centre experienced difficulty recruiting staff for unskilled posts. Thirty-five per cent of children at Geoffrey Field Junior School are currently eligible for free school meals: it is generally a higher percentage. Overall, Standard Assessment Tasks (SATs) results have been steadily improving and the 2000 PANDA (Performance and Assessment report) identifies the school's rate of improvement as being above the national average. Of the 89 Year 6 children assessed in 2000, the proportions achieving

Level 4 or above were English, 54 per cent; mathematics, 58 per cent; and science, 99 per cent.

The school's philosophy about raising attainment is clear, as is the strategy of target setting and detailed monitoring:

> When children join us in Year 3 from their infant schools, we look very closely at each child's attainment. As a basic principle, we believe that all the 2Cs and above should convert to at least Level 4s at the end of Key Stage 2, and the 2As and above to Level 5s. We focus on each child and set and review annually, specific and challenging targets for each one, including targets of Level 4 for some children who joined us below Level 2.
>
> (Headteacher)

The organization of the school is complex for an outsider to grasp, although all the children understand it well. The 320 children are organized into four year groups, each with three classes. Each year group occupies one of the four teaching wings, known as 'Areas' and designated by a colour (Blue: Year 3; Yellow: Year 4; Red: Year 5; and Green: Year 6). Each Area comprises what were originally three adjacent classrooms and a wide corridor. About 20 years ago, the windows between the classrooms and the corridor in each Area, as well as the classroom doors, were removed so that the corridor space could be used for teaching and resources and to facilitate teachers working cooperatively. The walls between the three classrooms have, to varying degrees, been demolished, as have some of the remaining low sections of wall between corridors and classrooms. The Green and Yellow Areas have also had a further classroom extension added. The effect is that the Areas are, to differing degrees, open. No classroom is enclosed.

One of the three teachers in each Area is the team leader. An experienced classroom assistant, known as a teaching facilitator, supports the work of each team. Teams operate to their own particular arrangements and schedules, but all set children across their three groups for literacy and numeracy on the basis of attainment and progress in that subject.

The school's approach to classroom organization

The idea of having spaces and furniture configured differently for different purposes is well established within Geoffrey Field Junior School. However, the ways in which this idea has translated into practice have changed, particularly following recent curriculum initiatives. Charlie Clare and his deputy, Jane Pearson, have encouraged Area teams to use their spaces strategically for a number of years. They have been conscious of the ways in which the classroom environment impacts on children's work and behaviour but, while providing a lead, have also been concerned that individual teachers and Area teams should exercise their professional judgements. However, over time, a common mode of operation developed throughout the school:

> We evolved and led people towards all having a studio,
> a maths workshop and a library. It was not us saying
> that you have to have it like that, it was showing how
> successful it was in one Area and then that spread out.
> Generally, that was thought to be the best pattern,
> and that was throughout the school . . . People took
> on board the idea of different scenarios for different
> purposes.
>
> (Headteacher)

An Area team would plan for the whole Area so that, during the course of any day, children moved between its three working spaces, according to the nature of the activity in which they were to be engaged:

> So teachers would book . . . Say they wanted to do a
> messy activity during the second session, they'd come
> to the art area [studio] for that session and those tables
> would generally be grouped. The middle space was
> generally a horseshoe and often the end space would be
> either grouped or a horseshoe. And teachers would have
> that in mind and book what they wanted and move
> around. An incidental advantage of that was that the

teachers left their spaces clear because it wasn't their
space. It was shared by the Area, by everybody.

(Deputy-headteacher)

This way of working ran well for two to three years until the
advent of the Literacy Hour in 1998 prompted discussion and, in
the end, changes to this way of working. Area teams wanted to
undertake the Literacy Hour simultaneously across all three teaching groups. Jane Pearson explained the changes:

But when the Literacy Hour, in particular, was introduced,
people wanted to do it at the same time as others. We felt
secure when it was being done at the same time . . . but
that was when we were obsessed with the egg timer, which
has gone now. That's how what we have got now started.
And then people wanted it with the Numeracy Hour. Well,
you definitely need to do the Numeracy Hour together,
more so than the Literacy Hour . . . So that is why there
has been a big change and that is why teachers have had
to find ways of changing spaces *within* their own space.

(Deputy-headteacher)

The school has therefore moved from having particular spaces
within each year group's Area configured to support different
types of activity. Although this worked well and to the school's
satisfaction, it could not accommodate the Literacy Hour or,
subsequently, the Numeracy Hour as it depended on the three
teachers in each team and the groups with which they were
working being engaged in different activities at any one time.
If all the teachers in an Area, or all the teachers across the
school, were to be implementing the Literacy Hour at the
same time, each needed to be working in a space and with
resources that supported the Literacy Hour activities. The existing arrangement simply could not accommodate this: it had
to change.

The Areas are now more class-based and there is less movement of children between classrooms within each Area. Indeed,
some teams of teachers have used furniture and display boards

to make clearer boundaries between the class teaching spaces. To begin with, a number of teachers returned to conventional group seating arrangements as their basic classroom layout. None stayed with this for long, however, finding that children were not sufficiently focused in whole-class teaching sessions or when asked to work on their own. The general pattern of practice throughout the school is still to match seating arrangements to task requirements, but this is now mostly done by changing seating arrangements within each teacher's space to match tasks, rather than moving children to differently configured spaces within an Area.

Staff at Geoffrey Field Junior School regard classroom organization, and seating configurations in particular, as an important pedagogical tool. But the four Area teams and the teachers within those teams differ in the approaches that they have developed and operate. In order to illustrate how things work 'on the ground', the work of teachers from three of the school's four Areas is now described.

Green Area: Year 6

The Year 6 base, known as Green Area, seems to be a good size when you see it first thing in the morning or at the end of the day. In contrast to Blue and Red Areas, Yellow and Green have had almost all vestiges of the walls that formerly defined three classrooms and a corridor removed: only pillars remain. The spaces are now L-shaped with the 'foot' formed by an extension added a few years ago. Once populated with the 93 Year 6 pupils, many approaching adult size, three teachers, the teaching facilitator and the LSA who work here, the impression changes. Although not cramped, little space remains unused (see Figure 3.1).

Julieanne Taylor, a teacher with about ten years' experience, leads the Green Area team. She prefers to work in the 'heel' of the 'L' so that she can see what's going on throughout her Area:

> Because I'm the coordinator, I've always argued the case for being in the middle. I like to see when I look up whatever is going on around me – who walks in, who

Key to all figures in the case studies

▨	Computers
▧	Walls and pillars
▢	Storage
▨	Moving tables
▨	Board

Scale

Figures 3.1 to 3.28　　　　　　　　　1m × 1m =

Figures 3.29 to 3.32　　　　　　　　1m × 1m =

walks out. And we have a newly qualified teacher in the Area so I want to be able to see and say 'Are you OK?', or to someone who's being a persistent pain, 'You! Over there!'

Julieanne joined the school when each Area was organized in three spaces, each for a different type of activity. However, she did not fully appreciate how this worked until well after she accepted the appointment. By then, things had begun to change to accommodate the Literacy Hour. What she already shared was the school's view that different classroom configurations were needed to support different types of learning activity. She attributes this to the fact that she had independently come to this conclusion as a pupil: 'I think [it was] because, as a child, I struggled and I hated interference'. At her previous school, where she taught in a small classroom that offered little scope for flexibility, she still managed to experiment to find arrangements that were practicable and supported particular types of activity and the attention they required, although this was not a practice adopted by the school as a whole: 'Sometimes the head would

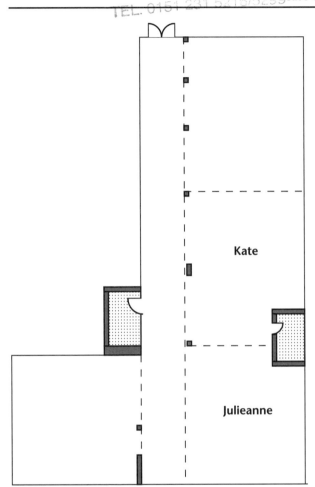

Figure 3.1 Green Area: Year 6. (Key on p. 56)

stop and say "Oh, you've moved the tables again", "Oh, this is
an interesting arrangement" . . . lots of comments like that, you
know.' Although not incurring disapproval, it seemed that her
experimental approach did not go unnoticed and prompted some
uncertain curiosity.

You do not need to spend more than a few minutes in Green
Area to appreciate that the team of three teachers, the teaching
facilitator and the LSA work to a highly organized programme.

Each teacher has their own base area and class but the children are in sets across the year for literacy and numeracy. For literacy there are three groups but for numeracy, Jane Pearson joins the team and the 93 children divide into four sets. Additionally, on two afternoons a week, and in preparation for SATs, maths booster sessions were operating. For these, Bradley Taylor joins the team, his work in Red Area being covered by his two colleagues, and the Green Area children form five differentiated sets.

Typically, as a day progresses and children move between groups and spaces for different activities, so some adjustment is made to seating arrangements to accommodate both changing numbers in each teacher's space and the nature of the lesson. At other times, groups move between different parts of the Area because a teacher and their class, or a subgroup, have work planned that requires use of the 'wet' area. As Julieanne summarized it:

> Children who are doing group activities or are being guided by their teacher work in groups. It's the same, generally, across the Area. You'll see that there are some groups and then some children arranged in individual ways, depending on the nature of the activity that they are going to do . . . children move from group desks to rows and children also move into all areas at different times.

It may appear complicated, but it is clear that the children know exactly what happens, when and why.

The way in which these teachers use classroom seating strategically is well illustrated in the work of Julieanne and one of her colleagues, Kate Parietti, the school's English coordinator. For example, in a numeracy session, Kate had just 22 children and arranged her area into three concentric arcs, with each row seating a subset, again differentiated by attainment in maths. She uses this 'amphitheatre' arrangement a good deal, finding that it supports whole-class teaching, individual and paired work (see Figure 3.2). Only when she wants children to work in groups of more than three does she ask them to put pairs of tables together and rearrange chairs (see Figure 3.3). But sometimes she will have her class seated on the floor immediately in front of the board for a whole-class session – for example, for a fast pace,

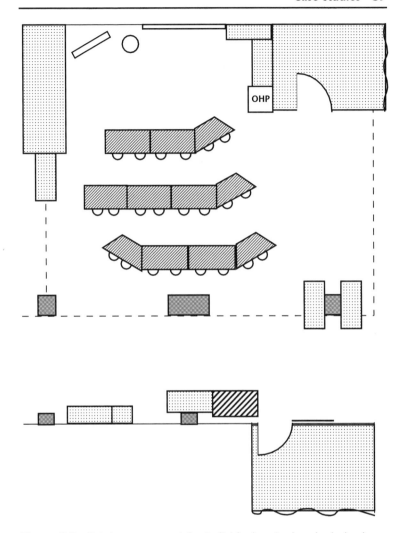

Figure 3.2 Kate's arrangement for individual, paired and whole-class work. (Key on p. 56)

highly interactive, ten minutes of 'mental maths', each child working with a marker and whiteboard, 'home-made' from laminated card. For this type of teaching she finds it easier to make frequent eye contact with everyone, to generate and maintain momentum and to sustain children's involvement.

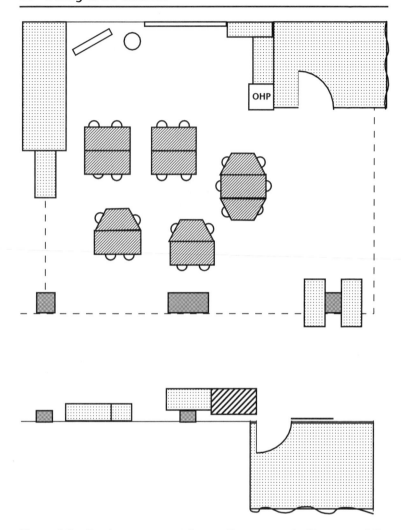

Figure 3.3 Kate's arrangement for small-group work. (Key on p. 56)

Julieanne Taylor also began her lesson with her group sitting on the floor, with a few at the back on chairs. For most of the lesson, however, children worked seated either in a horseshoe or at one of three group tables, at one of which the Area's teacher facilitator was based (see Figure 3.4).

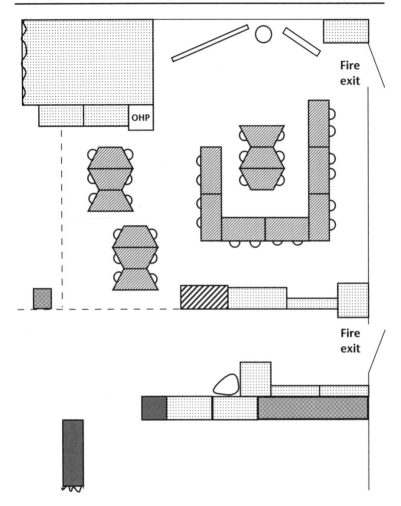

Figure 3.4 Julieanne's arrangement for individual, paired and whole-class work. (Key on p. 56)

Julieanne explained her rationale:

My children, who are pretty independent, sat in my horseshoe because I did not want them to talk. They had a pile of work to get through. I left a seat empty so that I could sit there. Then they moved up and I moved down a seat so that I had one-to-one with every child. I knew they were fine, but I wanted to push them harder. And then in my lowest attaining group, they are still at the stage where they need to talk about it and they need to be looking at what other people around the table are doing. And they need a bit of 'come on now, we can do this'. They need to be supported and have that 'we're all struggling but we're going to get there in the end' feeling and have the reassurance of others around them. My other group are beginning to find their feet and I think I'll be beginning to move them off and into a space of their own to consolidate . . . they have had a lot of support.

The practice of doing some whole-class sessions with children seated on the floor is partly a consequence of necessity. Being completely open, Green Area can get quite noisy, which makes it easy for children in one group to become distracted by another group's activities. The staff are very conscious of this. Indeed, with the increased amount of time now spent on whole-class teaching, the school has considered installing dividers to break up the Areas and dampen sound, though for the moment resources exclude the possibility. Julieanne would rather cope with this problem than have the space broken up and her capacity to fulfil her role as area coordinator constrained:

One of the things mentioned recently by our adviser was the carry-over of sound between teaching groups. I don't want barriers. It will reduce the light. It will reduce the support we give one another – like this morning there was one child [in another teacher's class] who does not know it yet but I'm going to catch up with him later to have a word about what I saw him doing . . .

Because she joins the team daily for numeracy, Jane Pearson knows the issues first hand and reinforced the way in which the team's organization is tailored not only to the task but also to accommodate the features of the space:

On a lot of the numeracy videos they have the whole-class teaching with the children at desks and really, in an ideal world, especially with Year 6 children, it is much better because they can have their equipment out in front of them. But the noise carry-over is too much, so we've got to pull them closer . . . There are always pay-offs, disadvantages and advantages. There are many advantages to being open but one of the disadvantages is the noise carry-over and the interactive teaching you get in numeracy can make it difficult . . .

For Julieanne and Kate, the layouts shown in Figures 3.2 and 3.4 represent the general form in which they configure their spaces for many activities. However, both they and their pupils adapt layouts with little fuss to suit the task and the numbers involved. When a major shift is needed (as shown in Figures 3.3 and 3.5), the children generally do the moving – but not always. Julieanne explains:

We've trained the children. They're quick, they're efficient and they're quiet. They know what to do and they know where to put things. But . . . sometimes, you're not going to stop to rearrange the furniture, in which case we'll [staff] all do it, or we'll get the children to stay and do it at lunchtime.

Discussing the way things work in Green Area with the Year 6 children was not easy. Although unusual to our eyes, moving furniture, as well as groups, was entirely familiar to the pupils – and not just since they had been in Green Area. Purposeful mobility had been normal for them since joining the school. For them, working in 'groups' meant sets and subsets as much as seating arrangements – although the two did not correspond: 'Normally, we're in groups [for maths]. Six in the front row and eight in the next . . . Group 1 in Mrs Taylor's group, they need more help'.

When thinking about how and why they worked best, and about which seating arrangements they preferred, children's comments showed that the relationships between classroom context, attention and behaviour had not eluded them:

I like to sit in groups . . . you can talk to other people.

. . . if you want to work on your own, you can go and sit over there . . . You can get on better because there's not so many people to talk to.

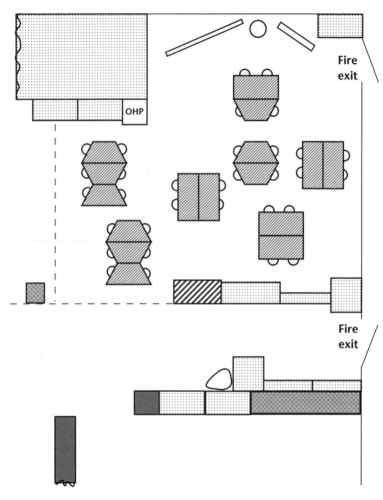

Figure 3.5 Julieanne's arrangement for small-group work. (Key on p. 56)

> I think . . . in a group [is best] because you can ask their opinions about work: 'Do you think I should do it this way or that?'

> I do more work sitting in a horseshoe.

The children were in no doubt about where the most interesting sessions took place. It was when the whole class was together as a unit, in this case on the carpet and focused on the teacher or classmates presenting: 'The teacher can speak with everyone . . . she gets to explain it to everyone . . . and they can hear'.

Blue Area: Year 3

The spring term of 2000 was Lesley Beaton's second term in her first full teaching job. Born and educated in South Africa, she trained and qualified in the UK and joined Geoffrey Field the previous September. The school's organization in Area teams and its approach to classroom organization were new to her on appointment, but she readily developed her own teaching as a member of the Year 3 team and became an increasingly enthusiastic advocate of both.

The three Blue Area teachers and one full-time teaching facilitator, led by Jane Morgan, work together in planning and, to a lesser degree, in practice. The three class groups of Year 3 children were put together on the basis of information, including Key Stage 1 results, from the adjoining infant school, from which most children have progressed. Lesley has the highest attaining group of 10 girls and 15 boys and occupies the middle teaching space of three adjoining classrooms, all linked by a long and open corridor area and through openings formed in the original dividing walls (see Figure 3.6). Her space is a good size with windows onto the large playground on one of the longer sides and an internal cloakroom for children's coats and bags. The classroom is equipped with wall-mounted display boards and a mobile whiteboard, an overhead projector, a screen and flipchart. Resources are stored along one wall beneath a display board, in the areas joining the two neighbouring classes and, to a limited extent, in the open corridor. Two computers on workstations nestle in one corner. The overall impression is airy, colourful, tidy and curriculum focused.

The children's furniture is a mix of 8 standard rectangular tables, with sides in the ratio 2:1, and 10 trapezoidal tables from the same range. Their chairs are light, stackable and metal framed, with blue-grey plastic seats and mid-back supports – similar to those found in many primary classrooms.

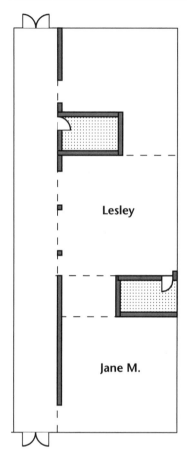

Figure 3.6 Blue Area: Year 3. (Key on p. 56)

Lesley thought a good deal about how she uses the space and resources available and tried a number of different configurations before settling on her current practice. This involves two main arrangements. The first (see Figure 3.7) has two 'horseshoes', one nested within the other, with an additional surface formed by three rectangular tables near the front of the classroom for a group of six children. There is also space for a further six children to sit as a group in the corridor area – usually with the teaching facilitator. The horseshoes have relatively short 'arms'

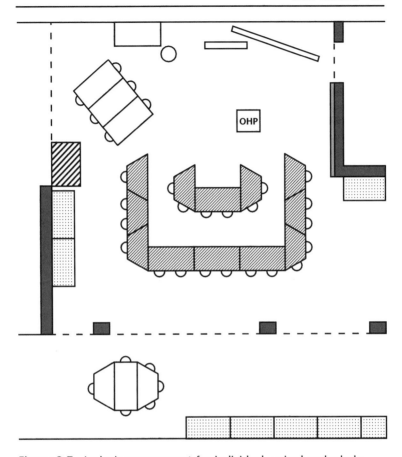

Figure 3.7 Lesley's arrangement for individual, paired and whole-class work. (Key on p. 56)

but the space between them allows Lesley to get to each child to work with them face to face. Compared with group seating, where teachers generally work over a child's shoulder from behind, Lesley finds that the horseshoe arrangement allows better eye contact and makes conversations more focused and fluent. It also seems to make it easier both to notice, and then quietly to deal with, children who are distracted: a meeting of eyes is often enough. Access to resources is helped by the provision of a number of 'carryalls' containing items such as pencils, crayons, rulers and erasers, each shared by four or five children.

This arrangement is how the day generally starts: it is used for the greater proportion of time, including literacy and numeracy teaching. However, each child does not have a set position, nor do they have a free hand in choosing neighbours. For literacy, the class is organized on the basis of five groups, broadly differentiated by attainment and named after a big cat (Tigers, Panthers, etc.). On each day of the week, one of these groups will sit at the group table where Lesley joins them for guided work: 'I like to work with one group on the very big table, so I'll say "Right Cheetahs, I want you today", so the Lions take their place.'

Most of the rest of the class sit in the 'horseshoes', often in an alternating boy–girl sequence which Lesley finds works well in sustaining work and attention when the children are meant to be working individually or in quiet pairs. A few, generally the Tigers, work with the teacher facilitator at the other group table, except when there are whole-class activities.

Numeracy works in much the same way, except that children are organized in four, rather than five, groups. Again, the groups are differentiated by rate of progress. The horseshoes, with two tables for groups working with the teacher or teaching facilitator, suit the mix of teaching for numeracy just as well as for literacy. However, they are not fit for all purposes, especially those where children need a large surface or the task requires discussion and collaboration in groups of more than two.

Lesley's second arrangement (see Figure 3.8) is more like a conventional primary classroom. Tables are reorganized to make larger surfaces for groups of four to six children. Although it is the task and not the curriculum subject that drives the decision to switch to the second arrangement, Lesley uses it more for science, geography and, to a lesser extent, history than for other subjects. As these subjects now tend to take place in the afternoon, the rearrangement often happens at lunchtime. Change from one configuration to another happens at most twice a day and is generally executed by monitors – a keenly sought position – whose proficiency is regularly demonstrated by turnaround times of rarely more than about 90 seconds.

These two seating arrangements seem to be able to accommodate all regular teaching and learning activities. Lesley's classroom is a good size and her children are relatively small. This

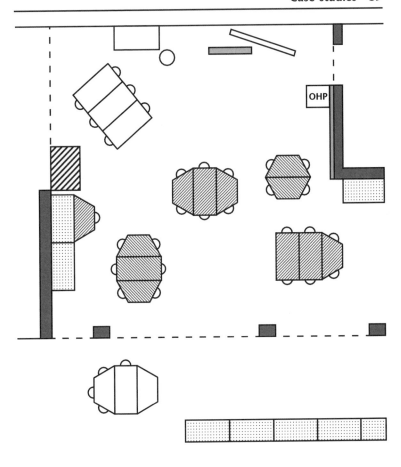

Figure 3.8 Lesley's arrangement for small-group work. (Key on p. 56)

combination means that she has the space to have the whole class sit on the carpet at the front of the room when she thinks it appropriate, and that is generally how the day starts for registration. From there, children sometimes move into activities in which the room is used in yet other ways. Although their teacher established the routines and inducted these children into the two classroom layouts, moving furniture and using space to support learning quickly became integral and unobtrusive aspects of normal classroom life for this class. For Lesley, it now seems an obvious way to work.

Red Area: Year 5

Red Area is the base for Year 5 (see Figure 3.9). As with the other Areas, it is where a team of three teachers, in this case led by Geoff Benson and a full-time teaching facilitator, work with their children. This year, the team has an exceptionally small cohort of 74. Bradley Taylor joined the Red Area team at the start of the

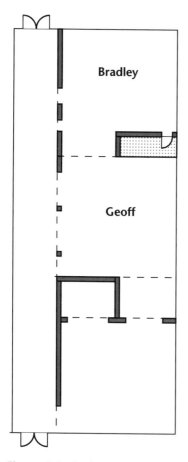

Figure 3.9 Red Area: Year 5. (Key on p. 56)

year. As a newly qualified teacher, his previous experience had been in schools with conventionally organized classrooms where children sat at grouped tables for all activities. Indeed, this was how he arranged his classroom when he began teaching at Geoffrey Field. He was conscious that not all his colleagues' classrooms operated like this, but it was following discussion at an in-service education and training (INSET) day that he developed his current practice:

> I must say, every single one of my teaching practices was in a school using grouped tables. There was some group work but . . . well . . . the task might have been differentiated for that group, but it was still an individual task. It just struck home straight away when someone said it.
>
> We ask children to do all these *individual* tasks and then put them in a social context . . . It happened more in maths actually, just lots of chatter and they make mistakes because people aren't concentrating – though in literacy as well. So this is why I have set it up . . . it's not that way any more.

Like Lesley in Blue Area, Bradley now has two main layouts – a horseshoe and grouped tables. The horseshoe (see Figure 3.10) has up to 22 children seated around the 'U' with a set of three tables in the centre, for a group of 6 to work with him. This supports individual work, paired activities and some whole-class teaching. However, Bradley will often have all his children seated on the floor in front of his board for whole-class sessions. This is not his preference but, as elsewhere in the school, a way of coping with the bleed of noise from one teaching space to the next:

> I suppose getting the children to sit on the floor . . . that's . . . the noise thing . . . I've not worked in an open plan school before; it was always enclosed classrooms . . . I never really know whether my kids are being quiet or whether its because they feed off other children's noise. So if Geoff's class are discussing or simply making a noise then, instinctively, the noise level in here goes up. Yet when they're quiet, I know mine can be quiet . . . children do focus in on the teacher that they listen to and they can, kind of, block out . . . [but] I do think you have to keep the pace of the lesson going, obviously.

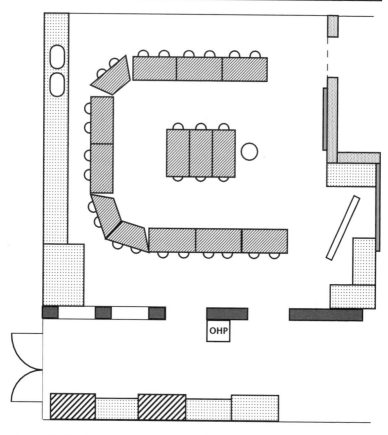

Figure 3.10 Bradley's arrangement for individual, paired and whole-class work. (Key on p. 56)

The activities of one morning well illustrate how Bradley now uses the space and different seating arrangements to support different teaching and learning activities.

The day begins with children in just two registration groups and a briefing for the children by the team leader, Geoff Benson, about a forthcoming trip to the Tower of London. Bradley has rearranged his area from its overnight horseshoe into five sets of grouped tables (see Figure 3.11). For literacy, he has the middle set of 22 children from Red Area, whom he again differentiates into three subgroups named, in descending order of current

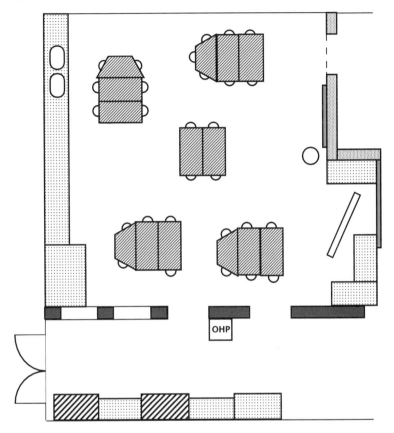

Figure 3.11 Bradley's arrangement for small-group work. (Key on p. 56)

attainment, Apostrophes, Hyphens and Commas. Arriving from the adjoining classroom, they settle on the floor immediately in front of the overhead projector beside which Bradley is sitting with the poem 'The Lady of Shalott' projected brightly on the screen behind him. The session is focused on narrative poetry and planned to support practice in reading verses and poems aloud with expression; understanding unfamiliar and uncommon words; using a dictionary; and identifying rhyming patterns. Children are invited to read a verse, following which Bradley reads it again and deconstructs each line. He pauses at unknown words, inviting the class to speculate on their meanings while a few children consult dictionaries and prepare to tell the class what they have found out. The session has pace and plenty of acknowledgements and recognition of contributions. After reading the whole poem and recapping on the unusual words, the rhyming pattern is discussed. This is difficult but the class works its way to a conclusion.

The next phase of the lesson has children working in groups reading a selection of comic verses and then each child in turn performing a verse to their group, paying attention to the rhyme to ensure that it remains funny. Bradley explains the membership of each group, appoints its task leader and, group by group, dispatches them with a caution to 'Watch how loud you are'.

He makes the transition to the final episode of this lesson, a spelling test of words learned for homework, by counting down ('OK now, 5, 4, 3, 2, 1'). Although it is an individual and silent task, it is brief and children stay sitting in groups. It is now breaktime and children follow the instruction to hand in their tests as they leave. Four have been asked to remain to rearrange the classroom into the horseshoe configuration ready for the numeracy session that follows break.

Bradley uses a good deal of paired work in literacy, frequently with more competent children working with less competent partners. The horseshoe configuration suits this, he finds. While he works with a group of children at the centre table, perhaps for guided reading or writing, pairs of children work around the horseshoe and he can easily keep an eye on what all are doing. The pairings often end up as being mixed by sex as well as by attainment:

> When I get the Apostrophes to work with the Commas or Hyphens, so the ability is mixed, I do get girl–boy because, let's face it, most of the Apostrophes are girls and most of the Commas are boys . . . Even the girls in my middle group [Hyphens] are at the top end of that group, rather than the bottom.

Paired work features much more frequently in Bradley's planning and teaching than cooperative tasks involving more than just two children. Consequently, he keeps the classroom in the horseshoe arrangement for most of the time: it suits every type of activity except those for which all need to be working in large groups simultaneously. It also allows him to work with a small group of children while others are getting on with paired or individual tasks, often following a whole-class introduction:

> I think numeracy and literacy lend themselves so well to whole-class work, especially when the year group is set in ability groups. Because the abilities of the children are fairly similar, I often differentiate the task by outcome, meaning the whole class are working towards a similar goal. In numeracy, for example, I often have the lower attaining ones in this group setting [in the centre of the horseshoe] because I often work with them.

Working with his classroom arranged in this way is still relatively new, but Bradley has no doubts so far about the advantages over standard group seating: 'Certainly in terms of time on-task [it's made a difference] and that's got to have an impact on their attainment. So, it's only been a little less than a month but "Yes", I really like working like this'.

A whole-school approach?

These teachers at Geoffrey Field Junior School all use the organization of their classrooms to support different teaching and learning goals, but not all in the same ways. In part these differences reflect the configuration of the spaces in which they each teach, but they are also the product of personal preferences, experiences and assessments of 'what works best for me and the children I teach'. What Charlie Clare and his staff share is informed conviction and experience that seating arrangements make a substantial difference to the ways in which their pupils work, behave and learn, and a desire to create environments that make it easier for children to progress and achieve.

Long Lane Primary School, Reading

It is rare to come across LEA primary schools in which group seating arrangements have not been the norm for at least 20 years. Long Lane Primary School, serving an area to the west of Reading in Berkshire, is an exception. Here, Key Stage 2 classes have had rows as their standard arrangement for as long as any existing staff can recall. However, the ways in which the school's teachers use their classroom layouts to support learning have changed in some respects in the last few years to accommodate developments in teaching literacy and numeracy.

With around 260 children on roll, most coming from privately owned homes, just 4 per cent of Long Lane's pupils are eligible for free school meals and 16 per cent have been identified as having special needs. Both figures are below the national averages. The recruitment profile is slightly unusual in that the school has a one class intake to the infant department, drawn from the immediate locality, and a second intake at the start of Key Stage 2 when a further class joins from a nearby infant school serving a slightly less affluent neighbourhood. Strong parental demand for places reflects Long Lane's reputation and standing in the community as a good primary school. Ofsted confirmed the quality of education provided following an inspection in May 2000: 'Long Lane is a good school. It is managed well and provides a very effective environment for learning. Pupils achieve well in their work and very well in their personal development. The quality of teaching is good' (Ofsted 2000: 7).

Key Stage 2 SATs results for English and science tend to be above national averages and better than those from similar schools, with annual variations running with the proportions of Year 6 pupils with special needs. In June 2000, 81 per cent of the 32 Year 6 pupils achieved Level 4+ in English and in science, and 63 per cent achieved level 4+ in maths. In the previous year the figures had been 94 per cent, 92 per cent and 68 per cent respectively, from a cohort of 51.

Tim Kuhles had been headteacher at Long Lane Primary School for seven years when we visited in the spring of 2000. Although initially unsure about the strategy of having Key Stage 2 children seated in rows, he was soon convinced of its merits and recognized that, in the eyes of many of the school's parents, this was a key component of the ethos and quiet working atmosphere within the school: 'Parents would riot if we changed it!'

Mike Lambden, the deputy-headteacher, who has been at the school a good deal longer, and who had responded to the letter we placed in *The Times Education Supplement*, reinforced the point: 'The parents are very happy . . . parents use it [rows] as a reason why their children need to come to this school. It is perceived as "the children are being taught properly".'

However, the approach that the school has taken has not been driven by parental expectation. There has been a clear and shared view among staff that, for the great majority of primary classroom teaching and learning activities, group seating arrangements are inappropriate. Indeed, because the school's practice of having rows as the basic form of classroom organization has been so well established, teachers applying for a job at Long Lane have needed to accept and feel confident about working that way. Mike elaborated:

Everyone who has passed through this school . . . has operated this kind of so-called 'formal arrangement'. We look on groups as 'old fashioned'. In fact, it would be a turn-off for us, if looking for another job, to go back to group arrangements . . . I don't accept the criticism that groups are the only way to handle differentiation. I can stimulate the able children and get around to see *all* children. With an interactive question and answer session, I can differentiate for individuals with the questions . . . [In rows] children can concentrate; they're not distracted; they're not twisted round or contorted in their seats and they can focus on their work. It just seems like common sense.

Although rows has been the norm across the school's Key Stage 2 classrooms for many years, teachers have also, to varying degrees, adapted their basic layout to suit different activities. Collaborative tasks for groups have not featured prominently in the school's curriculum and teaching methods. But some teachers have, over the years, had a different arrangement of classroom furniture for tasks where a large surface area is helpful – in art and technology, for instance. Typically, this has involved pushing the tables from two rows together.

Most of the children leaving Long Lane progress to the same 11–18 secondary school nearby. The impression that the staff and parents receive from the secondary school has reinforced confidence in Long Lane's practices and consolidated its reputation among parents. As the headteacher explained, the feedback that he gets is that the secondary school finds that his former pupils 'know what they are there for' and 'hit the ground running' in Year 7.

Implementing the NLS and NNS led the whole staff to consider how best to accommodate the recommended teaching activities within their well established practices and convictions. Again the headteacher explained:

> Some of these traditions predate my arrival at the school seven years ago, but one of the things I liked about the school when I was viewing it was that . . . it matched how I perceived things working to the best interests of children. When literacy and numeracy came in, the concept of whole-class teaching was already firmly established. We weren't a school that believed in 'integrated day', 'group work' – that kind of stuff that I was taught to do at college!

Although already accustomed to a greater than average use of whole-class teaching, the school has made two related changes to accommodate the literacy and numeracy curricula. First, there was unease about national recommendations for guided reading:

> We made a policy when the Literacy Strategy came in. Having tried it, in our view it was not possible to do justice to guided reading within the hour. We just said, 'We don't think we can do this'. Maybe we're not good enough, but we don't perceive that we'll have the time to do justice to guided reading within the hour. And we are not going to play at it. So we created another 20 minutes before lunch which is specifically for guided reading: that is, every day. So then we said to ourselves, 'OK, how do we actually arrange the furniture to facilitate that, bearing in mind the dreadful slippage that can occur in terms of time if you are faffing around with furniture?'
>
> (Headteacher)

The answer, generated by two of the staff and now adopted in all but one of the Key Stage 2 classrooms, was to rearrange the classroom to have one group table, known in the school as the 'focus table'. Within each class, children belong to one of five focus table groups – one for each day of the week. In the period when we visited the school, Tim Kuhles was teaching a Year 5 class for two days a week and illustrated how this worked for his class:

> I teach on a Tuesday and a Thursday. So, take my Tuesday group as an example. When the children come in on a Tuesday they know they get their bits and pieces and come and sit at the focus table with me. So wherever they normally sit, other children will be in those places. When the Literacy Hour is going on, and they are coming up to the independent work, I will concentrate on those children: my focus is on that. Then at guided reading time, of course, the pattern is established. They come straight back from maths and Wallop! . . . you're into your guided reading with a carousel of activities for the other named day groups.

The only teacher who does not now arrange his classroom with a focus table is Mike Lambden, the deputy-headteacher. The reason for this exception relates entirely to the size of his classroom and the fact that he has Year 6 children, who, unsurprisingly, tend to be the largest in the school. As explained later, although he does not have a focus table arranged as group seating, he does operate a 'day groups' system, like Tim Kuhles and the other Key Stage 2 teachers.

The second organizational change the school made to accommodate literacy and numeracy teaching has been setting children for literacy and numeracy. At first, setting for literacy was introduced on the basis of attainment and *across* year groups. However, this has been revised and now setting for literacy and numeracy is done across classes but *within* the same year group.

A third recent development, which has nothing to do with literacy or numeracy teaching requirements, but which well reflects the attention that the school gives to the conditions in which it asks pupils to learn, has been the acquisition of new furniture. After a good deal of investigation, and with valuable support from parents, a range of ergonomically designed chairs, manufactured in Australia, was identified and bought for most of the classrooms. From the school's viewpoint, the benefits have been multiple: improved concentration, less fidgeting, more work and, quite simply, more comfortable children. These beneficial effects have left governors in no doubt that, immediately funds become available, the remaining sets of conventional chairs should be replaced.

There is, then, a much greater degree of consistency evident in the approach to teaching and to classroom organization across the Key Stage 2 classes at Long Lane than in most schools. Indeed, the way in which the classroom environment has been organized, in what some would see as 'old fashioned rows', seems to have been one of the school's most appealing characteristics for parents. However, this has not proved to be an ossified convention as the staff have adapted their approach to accommodate the types of teaching and learning activities encouraged through recent changes in the teaching of literacy and numeracy. What has remained evident is a concern to create physical environments within classrooms that support learning.

How this works 'on the ground' can be seen by briefly considering the work of three teachers and their classes.

Anne Stopforth: Year 3

Anne Stopforth entered teaching as a newly qualified teacher (NQT) in September 1999, having completed her training as a mature student at a nearby higher education institution. Two aspects of her training course led her to apply for a post as teacher of a Year 3 class at Long Lane, knowing that she would be comfortable working within its ethos and classroom approach.

First, as part of her initial training course Anne completed a two-week school placement in which her work focused on group work and collaboration between children for learning. This experience highlighted for her the relationships between tasks and seating arrangements and the differences between group work, group seating and grouping for curriculum and differentiation purposes. In particular, it set her thinking about the suitability of grouped seating for work that did not entail groups of children collaborating. The second aspect was the fact that she had successfully undertaken a teaching practice placement in the school and was therefore already familiar with the school's policy, had experience of working within it and had liked it. She was successful in her application and was appointed to teach the 26 children forming one of the school's two Year 3 classes.

Anne's classroom is long and relatively narrow, measuring about 4m by 9m. Unlike most classrooms, which tend to have their door near a corner, you enter Anne's right in the middle of one of its long sides (see Figures 3.12 and 3.13). This rather unusual configuration is a consequence of the original, roughly square, room being extended to almost double its area. Natural light enters through windows along most of the other long wall. These architectural features impose their own limitations on the range of possibilities for organizing the classroom. There is also the need to accommodate not only materials, resources, computers and printers used by her class, but also the school's recently acquired stock of mini-computers and their recharging unit for which, as the school's information and communication technology (ICT) coordinator, Anne has responsibility.

The layout that Anne has evolved and which she uses for most activities is shown in Figure 3.12. Eighteen children sit at nine tables arranged in the form of a slightly exploded 'E', with most of them directly facing a movable whiteboard. On the other side of an invisible corridor running between the classroom entrance and the fire exit sit a further six children at a focus or 'guided group' table. Just behind them are the remaining two places. Within this layout, children are seated in pairs with a same-sex partner.

This configuration is used for most activities in which the task is individual or involves pairs working together, and for some whole-class teaching sessions. For guided reading and other occasions when Anne needs to work with just a group, the children who have the focus table as their base will swap places with those whose turn it is to work with their teacher.

As an alternative to using this layout for whole-class teaching and discussions, Anne will occasionally have the whole class gathered on the carpet in the resource base end of the classroom. This is only a viable option because it is a Year 3 class of 7- and 8-year-olds. Larger children simply would not fit into the space. However, even with relatively small children, the limited space

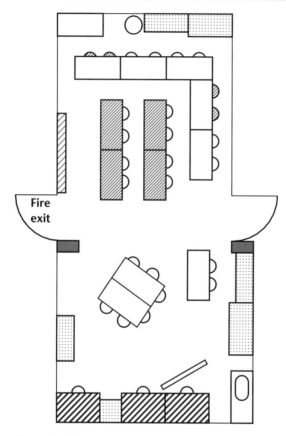

Figure 3.12 Anne's arrangement for individual, paired and whole-class work. (Key on p. 56)

within the classroom means that movement has to be carefully managed and orchestrated. For example, when returning to their seats from a discussion or briefing on the carpet, children are 'dispatched' in named groups or 'prongs' of the 'E'. For the same reason, Anne tends to ask one member of each side of the 'E' and of the focus table to get books and resources for the other children in order to restrict the amount of movement within the classroom.

The limited space within this classroom and its unusual shape again impose limitations and restrict the possibilities for moving furniture to create a supportive environment for group work. So,

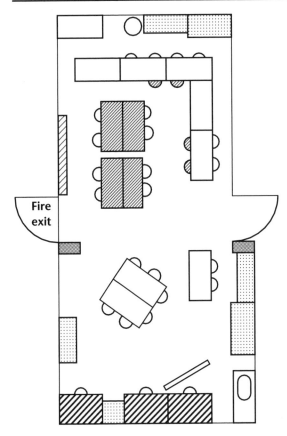

Figure 3.13 Anne's arrangement for small-group work. (Key on p. 56)

instead of moving too many tables, the class has a system in which just four tables move and eight children shift themselves and their chairs to create three working groups of four and two of six (see Figure 3.13). The remaining pair sometimes work together or also move to join a group. Some of these groups are working around single tables, an arrangement which might prove problematic with older and longer-legged youngsters. Moving between their regular layout and this one is a well practised and efficiently conducted routine that usually happens at lunchtime, break or the end of the day. However, given that the most teaching activities are accommodated within the normal seating arrangements, the shift to the group work format happens only a few times each week.

By and large, Anne is pleased with the two layouts that she has developed for use with her Year 3 class to support their learning within this less than spacious and less than optimally shaped classroom. Moreover, her children understand and entirely accept the rationale for, and the sense of, the two set-ups. But the 'E' configuration has also had an unintended and unexpected consequence. It seems that the four sides of the 'E' have developed identities as groups and, as with all groups, within-group cohesion and cooperation is matched, and to some extent supported, by between-group competition. This is a dynamic that Anne finds she can sometimes use to good effect in her teaching, though carefully!

Catherine Foley: Year 4

Teaching a class of children who are all facing the front and seated in rows has never seemed unusual for Catherine Foley, Long Lane's maths coordinator. She joined the school as an NQT four years ago but only learned of its approach to teaching and classroom organization at interview. .However, by chance, she had completed one of her four teaching practices as a student in a school that operated in a similar manner to Long Lane and had felt quite relaxed about it.

Her class of 29 Year 4 children occupies a classroom providing a 7m square working area. To one side of it, and separated by a half-height wall bearing sinks, is a cloakroom area for coats and bags. Two computers and storage are arranged along the rear wall: on the front wall a whiteboard is mounted. Sorting out which is the back and the front of this classroom, as with all in Long Lane, is not difficult as the normal arrangement has the children seated facing 'the front'. Catherine Foley is quite clear about her rationale:

> Really, I think if we are setting ourselves up to say that teaching isn't about facilitating, its about teaching and you are the focus. They [children] need to be sat so that they can focus on you – and not on what the child opposite them is doing.

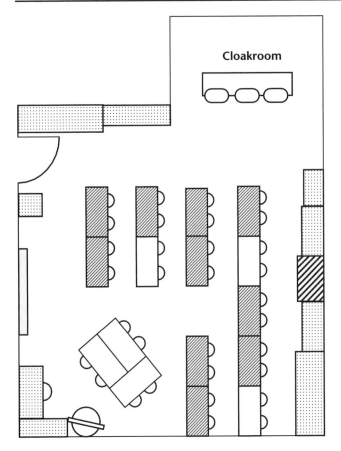

Figure 3.14 Catherine's arrangement for individual, paired and whole-class work. (Key on p. 56)

As Figure 3.14 shows, there is one long row of tables at the back of the classroom for ten children, four shorter rows of four and a group table at which six can sit. Catherine finds that this layout gives her access to everyone. Until recently all the furniture was arranged in rows. Along with most of the other Key Stage 2 teachers, she introduced a 'focus table' to support developments in literacy and numeracy teaching. In fact, the concept of a focus table might have begun in her classroom:

I was finding it very hard to focus on the group of children without a real place for them to go, so it was harder for reading and writing . . . and particularly for maths, so I wanted to put them together so that I could have a focus . . . I think I triggered it actually because there were all rows on this side of the school. I changed mine and then Mrs Thorne [Year 5] said 'Oh yes, we can do that' so we have kind of built it up.

The constraints of space require that some children sit at the focus table even when it is not being used for that purpose. Catherine tends to have 'the more "wobbly" ones who need a bit more support' based there at such times. However, for guided reading and writing, a different group will gather there with her each day.

It's the same with maths. Some maths lessons they will come in and say 'Who's sitting on the group table?' Some days it doesn't really matter as it's more a whole-class lesson. Some days I will try to place the most able children there because I find it difficult to make myself focus on them. Then I know I'm really going to sit down and try to extend them. It's quite informal day-to-day matter . . . I do it from my marking as well. If from my marking I think 'Oh right!: these children have not understood', they will become the focus group for the next day.

So, although the focus group table was introduced specifically to support guided work in literacy and numeracy teaching, Catherine now uses it and the strategy of working with a subgroup of the class for a variety for purposes. This necessarily means children changing seats, especially those for whom the group table is their base. They seem to have adapted reasonably well, even though their possessions and resources are in drawers under 'their desks':

Yes, that's the down side. That's the bit that I'm not sure I have really cracked, but I can't see a solution to it . . . I have actually been impressed with how well they have coped with it. When I tried this first I thought I'd try it for a week. I had visions of trying it and then giving up and going back to rows. We're still here. So they coped.

Although rows has been the school norm, Catherine also experimented with other arrangements. Having recently taken on the role of leading maths teacher in the LEA, she followed the suggestion within the NNS and experimented with a horseshoe arrangement similar to those used in some of the other classrooms described in this chapter. She did not take to it:

> I did try it. But you have to be able to visualize yourself
> in the classroom and no matter how much I did, I just
> couldn't see it. I do like to walk around in circles when
> I'm teaching – which I probably shouldn't – and with that
> sort of shape I just felt 'boxed in' in the middle: I just
> couldn't see it working.

Catherine finds that the rows and one group layout that she and her colleagues have evolved works pretty well. However, she does not have her children seated like this for all activities. Often they work together in pairs, but when she wants groups to work together, furniture and children will move. However, contrasting her approach to that of colleagues who have a second, well practised, configuration into which the class moves, Catherine is more informal and expects her children to find a practicable solution:

> I tend to do it quite informally . . . I just tend to plan a
> lesson and think 'Oh yes. They'd be better in groups'.
> Then I'll say that, so they just stand up and move: they
> just pick up their chairs and move . . . I just say 'You
> think about it', because I want them to think for
> themselves.

Sometimes alternate rows simply turn their chairs and join those sitting behind them. When a larger surface is needed, an arrangement such as that shown in Figure 3.15 appears.

For some whole-class teaching, briefing or discussion sessions, the whole class will come together at the front. Introducing the focus table has reduced the open carpet area – not that these children objected as they are none too keen on sitting on the floor. However, there are times when gathering closer together is appropriate, or even essential. On these occasions, some will

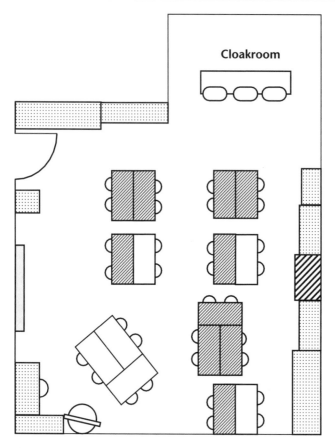

Figure 3.15 One of Catherine's arrangements for small-group work. (Key on p. 56)

sit on the floor and others on nearby chairs and tables. Sometimes, all the desks are pushed back to allow an amphitheatre of chairs.

In this classroom, there is no standard alternative to the basic layout although the space and furniture is certainly used flexibly and purposefully to support different types of activity. However, the possibility of never, or only very rarely, planning for collaborative learning involving more than pairs is well recognized by Catherine:

The majority of the research is that children don't work in groups: they simply do individual activities with the teacher cheerfully thinking they are working in groups because they are sitting in groups. So I think 'Why pretend?' If they are doing individual or parallel activities then I would rather have them in that situation. But you do have to make sure that you plan in a few group activities, so you plan an art lesson or a science lesson which really involves having five or six people with different roles. So one's got the stopwatch, one's got the thermometer and one's got the ice – so they have to work together. Because that is the other side, of course. You do need to develop those things and it is easy to forget this when you get thinking in rows. You have to make a conscious effort to plan those things in.

Four years into her teaching career, Catherine is very comfortable with and committed to her way of teaching. But she is also interested in broadening her experience and, when she progresses to another school, thinks she may well try group seating – just to see how it goes:

I am aware that I have only taught properly in a school where they sit in rows. So, for my development, I would actually want to make myself work for a while in a situation where they work in groups because it is a different dynamic and just to convince myself that I *could* work that way. But I think that then I would be drifting back to this system!

Mike Lambden, deputy-headteacher: Year 6

The pedagogical practices of Long Lane owe a good deal to the influence of Mike Lambden, its long-standing deputy-headteacher. From early in his career he departed from the norm of organizing his class in groups, believing that for most types of activity an arrangement in which all the children sat facing forward was more suitable. His first experience as a teacher was the spur: 'The head had taken all the doors off and designated areas for

English, art and maths. Children were free to go anywhere they wanted. I couldn't stand it, so an old timer, another teacher and myself started to change our arrangements.'

Then, in the mid-1980s, Mike read some of the earliest British research on the effects of group and row seating arrangements and became yet more secure in his commitment to this approach and to its development within Long Lane. Although his rows arrangement has attracted some politely critical interest among fellow teachers over the years, Mike argues its merits with vigour. He has encountered no problems:

> . . . other than in the past with assumptions in government
> documents that all children sit in groups. As for the
> students we have had in, much of their documentation
> has suggested that children will be in groups so when we
> have students on teaching practice, we have to negotiate
> with their tutors. We've had no problems with the
> students themselves.

The 32 Year 6 children in Mike's 'millennium class' work in a classroom of similar proportions to Catherine Foley's and, in common with all the classrooms at this end of the school, it has a partially separated cloakroom area to one side. It seems a good deal smaller than the others, but this is because there are more children and, being in Year 6, they are larger and have appropriately-sized tables. As a direct and unavoidable consequence, there is not enough room for a 'focus table', as used in the other Key Stage 2 classrooms. Instead, all the children sit in one of four forward-facing rows, with each row constructed from four, two-person desks (see Figure 3.16). The tables are modern, with suspended drawers in which children keep their personal resources, and the chairs are of the Australian, ergonomic design mentioned earlier. Seating positions start on the basis of pupils' choices, although the outcome is always subject to modification if any combinations seem to produce trouble or if a particular need arises.

Although there can be no focus or group table, this rows arrangement does not prevent Mike operating a 'day group' system for literacy, as in other classes. The difference is that today's day group will move to the back row and Mike will work with them there – as a group but in a row. The system works smoothly.

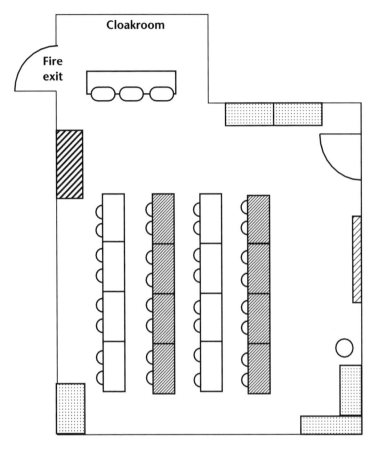

Figure 3.16 Mike's arrangement for individual, paired and whole-class work. (Key on p. 56)

Collaborative work in pairs and threes can be done in rows but when more than three need to get together some furniture shifting becomes necessary. If it is just for a discussion, the front and third row turn their chairs and join the row behind them. However, when a larger worksurface is needed, for instance for some art, technology and science activities, a more complex and well-drilled routine kicks in. It begins with everyone sitting in the first and third rows picking up their chairs and carrying them to the side of the classroom where they put them down and sit

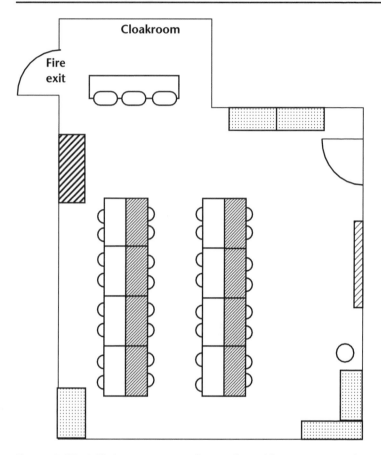

Figure 3.17 Mike's arrangement for small- and large-group work. (Key on p. 56)

down in a line, at right-angles to the tables, as spectators to the next move. The children in rows two and four then turn the tables in the first and third rows and push them up against their own to make two wide 'banquet' tables, and sit down again. The turning is necessary because of the drawer under each table. Finally, the spectators pick up their chairs again and take them to their new places at the 'banquet' (see Figure 3.17). What could easily be a time consuming and shambolic transition is neither of these. The exercise takes about a minute and is orderly and good humoured, but it is a major upheaval. However, Mike arranges the curriculum so that this change happens at the start or end of a session and only once or twice a week.

The school's approach

These three cases indicate a clear whole-school approach at Long Lane but also how each teacher tailors it to suit the area and configuration of space in which they work and their own purposes and preferences. While the other schools and teachers mentioned in this chapter have come to their current practice from the norm of group seating, Long Lane has approached it from a tradition of organizing classrooms in rows. At least this is how it has operated in its Key Stage 2 classrooms. The Key Stage 1 classes, however, tend to use group seating arrangements. In discussion, Tim Kuhles, the headteacher, explained that the consensus across the school was that this was a more appropriate approach for the youngest pupils, although the rationale for the difference in strategy between the two key stages is not fully articulated within the school. However, knowledge and understanding of the way the school uses classroom organization to support teaching and learning objectives is not only well established within the school but also among its pupils' parents.

Carnarvon Primary School, Bingham

The appointment of Lesley Molyneux as deputy-headteacher at Carnarvon, a ten-class primary school in the busy East Midlands market town of Bingham, proved to be a real catalyst for change. Two years on, four of the school's six Key Stage 2 classrooms now use flexible seating arrangements. All employ a form of 'horseshoe' or 'U-shape' arrangement along with other 'letter-shaped' formations such as Ls and Ts.

Lesley initially started using 'horseshoes', as she describes them, as part of her working practice at her previous school when they introduced the NLS a year early:

'Visibility' quickly became an issue when I was
implementing the strategy, particularly when I was
working with big books etc. It was so easy to lose children
in a group that I started to use a 'horseshoe shape' so I
could have eye contact with everyone and gauge their
responses.

At that time she was teaching in a small, three-class village
school, so her class was mixed and included children from Years
2, 3 and 4. She started to use the horseshoe shape and this
approach was soon picked up and used by the Year 5 and 6
teacher and then by a Reception, Year 1 and Year 2 colleague. In
effect, it quickly became a whole-school approach, with children
readily accommodating the routines of moving tables and chairs:
'Despite the mixed ages in my class, I didn't have any problems
with the youngest children moving the furniture. I just think it's
all down to how you train them to do it.'

The headteacher at Carnarvon, Linda Hunter Wallace, was
uncertain when Lesley joined the school about whether changing classroom seating arrangements was compatible with good
primary practice:

Initially, I felt it went against my understanding of what
constituted a lively, buzzing primary classroom and
against all my training and experience as a teacher. I felt
it would be like stepping back in a time warp. But I was
prepared to give time, opportunity and space for my new
'dynamic deputy' to demonstrate these aspects of her
practice.

Other factors also influenced Linda's acceptance and subsequent endorsement of Lesley's practice. She witnessed Lesley's
work, tried teaching in different classroom formats herself and
learned of research on classroom organization:

In the end, I felt three elements came together to convince
me. Firstly, I was able to do informal observations of
Lesley and see the arrangements in action. Secondly, I
was able to teach in the class as cover for Lesley. I really

enjoyed it because I felt as though I was a real teacher and not a minder. And finally I felt the research evidence added further weight to the argument.

In addition, the experience of introducing the NLS and NNS prompted further reflection on the appropriateness of group seating as standard practice. As a result, Linda Hunter Wallace initiated discussions with staff and then sent a letter to parents telling them that the school would be initiating changes in some of its classrooms. She included some statistical evidence and, to allay any fears, offered the assurance that there would be careful monitoring and changes would be made if necessary.

Two or three parents were concerned about the changes and wrote expressing their disquiet. Their concerns were that the changes:

- were going against the ethos of the school, which encouraged collaboration;
- might have health and safety implications in terms of escaping in a fire;
- must be the result of the school having a behaviour problem.

These concerns were addressed by asking for feedback from the teachers and inviting the parents to come into the school to view the arrangements. The parents involved were all well acquainted with the school, having had more than one child in their family attend Carnarvon. No concerns arose among the parents of children in Lesley's class however. By then they had experience of their children being taught in this manner and their comments were 'it's great' and, perhaps less reassuringly, 'more traditional'.

The use of flexible seating arrangements is now normal practice across most of the school's Key Stage 2 classes and the headteacher sees real differences in progress and attainment. She sees a greater degree of consistency between classes and has noticed that this enables supply teachers to fit in more readily and also to work more effectively. There have been no further expressions of uncertainty from parents in classes where practice has changed. The school has not, however, encouraged its Key Stage 1 teachers to follow their Key Stage 2 colleagues. The school's view is that speaking and listening in small groups in Key Stage 1 is of greater significance, and concern that small children may have difficulties moving the furniture justifies different practices in the two key stages.

Before turning to examine in more detail how some of Carnarvon's Key Stage 2 teachers use the organization of their classrooms to support teaching and learning, a broader consideration of the school and its setting may be useful. Overlooking fields, the school was built on the edge of, and at the same time as, an estate of private houses in the growing, but still relatively small, market town of Bingham. In addition to Carnarvon, Bingham boasts a further infant school and junior school, as well as a comprehensive school serving the town and neighbouring villages.

Carnarvon is single storey in design, with a semi-open plan main building and a more comprehensively open-plan annexe. The continuing growth of the town's population and housing is reflected at the school where an additional classroom has just been built. By the summer of 2000, the school had 11 classes, 5 for Key Stage 1 and 6 for Key Stage 2. Of the Key Stage 2 classes, 4 work in the main building and two in the annexe, each with about 30 children drawn from two year groups. In addition to teaching staff, the school employs six Learning Support Assistants (two full-time and four part-time), all with responsibilities for identified children with special needs. More support staff were to be recruited and three more classrooms were planned for completion in Summer 2002.

The school has a good reputation in its community for children's progression and attainment. Of the 48 Year 6 children assessed in 2000, the proportions gaining Level 4+ were 92 per cent (83 per cent) in English, 85 per cent (79 per cent) in maths and 98 per cent (95 per cent) in science. (Figures in brackets are for the 38 children assessed in 1999.) Of this cohort, 16.7 per cent was registered as having special educational needs. Key Stage 2 results have been consistently above national averages and also consistently improving since 1998. Parents' assessment of the quality of education provided and of the leadership of the school was endorsed by Ofsted which inspected Carnarvon in May 2000 and concluded that the quality of teaching was 'very good overall'. The headteacher's leadership was assessed as 'excellent'. Indeed, the whole tone of the report makes clear that the inspection team was enormously impressed by all that it observed and learned at Carnarvon.

Turning again to the way in which some of the school's Key Stage 2 teachers use classroom organization within their overall teaching strategies, the work of two has been selected for more detailed description. Although working in classrooms with similar spatial properties, the two teachers – Lesley Molyneux and Liz Wood – have developed different approaches.

Lesley Molyneux: Years 5 and 6

For most activities, Lesley's class sit in two horseshoes, one inside the other, with girls and boys sitting alternately (see Figure 3.18):

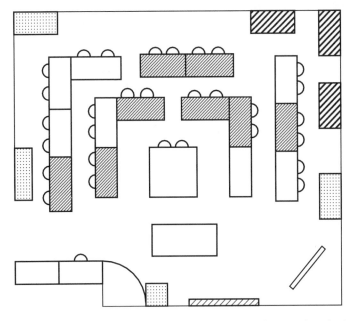

Figure 3.18 Lesley's arrangement for individual, paired and whole-class work. (Key on p. 56)

When I first arrived, it was obvious that gender was a real
issue in the school. There are 26 children in the class with
a large proportion of boys – something like 18 to 8. This is
why I started organizing the horseshoe so the seats were
sorted into boy/girl/boy/boy/girl etc. I feel the boys really
benefit from being with the girls and I try to ensure the
girls don't lose out either, by moving the boys round by
two places every term. That way when they work in pairs
they get to work with different people throughout the
year.

A successful career in commerce preceded Lesley's entry to
teaching. From the outset, the limitations of sitting children in
groups seemed to her to be as self-evident as the merits of her
horseshoe arrangement. A group of four of her children confirmed her expectation that they too appreciated the effects of
different seating positions on their behaviour and work:

I sometimes work with people I'm not too friendly with,
because my friends . . . I don't really get on well with work
with my friends . . . I don't work as well. 'Cos you spend a
lot of your time with them at play times and . . . they talk
too much . . . you like to be on your own in your
classroom . . .

I don't really like the horseshoe but I work better like that,
'cos there's not many people that you can actually talk to,
like if you sit in tables . . .

'Cos you can see everyone but you can't really talk to
them.

And you can all see the front . . . you can all see
everywhere.

At the beginning of term the boys sat in every other seat
and the girls didn't have to choose. Mrs M just said sit
there, sit there and that's how it happened . . . it's boy/girl,
boy/girl.

For paired, individual and whole-class work the horseshoe
arrangement is used, but for group investigations in maths,

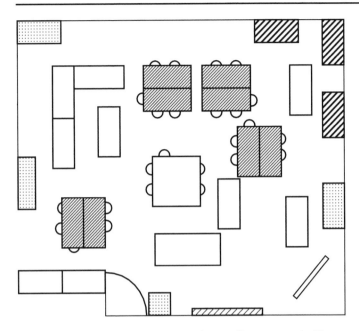

Figure 3.19 Lesley's arrangement for small-group work. (Key on p. 56)

science or technology children move either the tables or themselves: 'It's independent work when we're in the horseshoe but when we move the tables or we'll gather round one table, that's like when we do group work or gather round the computer.'

The change from the usual arrangement of two horseshoes into groups involves pushing one table from the inner horseshoe to join one from the outer to form a square (see Figure 3.19). For art, larger blocks of four tables are put together, making rectangles, and for debates all the tables are placed to the sides of the room and the chairs move to the centre. As a result, the children know a number of different arrangements which are used regularly.

The moves themselves are relatively painless. Each arrangement has a well understood name, such that Lesley refers to the 'left side of both horseshoes' or 'the inner horseshoe', for example, when setting children off to undertake tasks or dismissing them for lunch. During an observed session the class started in the familiar horseshoe arrangement but were then told to move into groups. Everyone was involved and the transformation took 55 seconds until all were either sitting down or preparing resources for the task in hand.

In practice, the double horseshoe is used for most lessons, with other arrangements used, on average, about three times in a week. Lesley had noted an early NLS document suggesting an alternative horseshoe, where the children sat inside the 'shoe' to work on their own, turning their chairs to face the teacher and board when necessary. A former colleague had tried this successfully but Lesley prefers her children to sit on the 'outside', primarily because of this arrangement's potential to support whole-class interaction as well as individual and paired work:

> I still maintain the advantages of the horseshoe arrangement centre around visibility and therefore around class control. If all the children can see me, the overhead projector and the board, and I can make eye contact with all the children, it's easier to see who is or is not responding and whether that response is appropriate. The children are more on-task because of this visibility. In particular, I can make eye contact from anywhere along the front of the classroom. I sometimes use a square table at the centre of the horseshoe, either for demonstration purposes or for setting out worksheets for collection.
>
> I really feel the arrangements do affect my ability to control the whole group and I feel I talk *to* the children rather than *at* them. It's also possible to take on their feedback and enable them to model tasks as well.

Summarizing her experience, Lesley views the practices that she and her colleagues have evolved as a rational progression from earlier conventions for classroom organization, and certainly not as a reversion to past practice:

> The arrangements have changed collaborative work minimally and reduced it to some extent, but then much of what was seen as group work was not really *collaborative* group work.
>
> I don't think I can fault the horseshoe arrangement, though obviously if I had a smaller classroom it might not lend itself to such flexible arrangements. In terms of

working with individual children, having the desks in an inner and outer horseshoe means I can sit alongside or work with a child from in front or behind. I've also used a traditional 'row' arrangement when doing 'The Victorians', but I think there was a downside to this, in that the classroom looked so formal and the children couldn't see one another, which didn't exactly lend itself to class interaction or feedback.

Liz Wood: Years 3 and 4

Liz Wood's classroom is slightly smaller than that of her colleague Lesley. So are her pupils – a mixed class of 30 Year 3 and Year 4 children. She too has a basic arrangement that is changed to suit particular types of activity, as and when necessary. To make best use of the space available to her and to meet her objective of having easy eye contact with every child when she is at the front of her classroom by the whiteboard, Liz has developed a layout using pairs of tables configured in L-shapes (see Figure 3.20). At the centre of the room, however, eight children work at the ends of four tables drawn together to make a large, rectangular surface. This layout preserves a carpet area on which the whole class can be gathered.

This arrangement came about through a process of experimentation. A number of different configurations were tried and tested for feasibility, effect and acceptability to Liz herself, to her children and to their parents. Rows was one of the possibilities tried, but it failed on several counts: 'I found the parents weren't comfortable with this. They felt rows made the classroom more formal and cold. In addition it seemed to be harder to move the rows . . . and it took longer.'

In time, the present and now established layout of L-shapes and a block evolved as her preferred option. It supports children working on their own and in groups, without too much distraction, as well as whole-class teaching and discussion. It also enables Liz to work with a group of children by having them swap places with those already sitting at the central block. However, when an activity requires the whole class to be working in groups, or when larger surfaces are needed, rearranging the L-shapes into

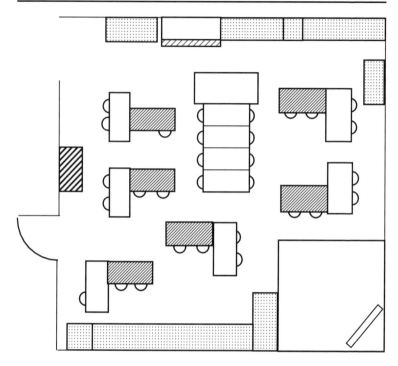

Figure 3.20 Liz's arrangement for individual, paired and whole-class work. (Key on p. 56)

squares entails just six tables moving, as shown in Figure 3.21. As in other classrooms at Carnarvon, the move itself is a well-rehearsed and polished operation. Changing from the basic lay-out to groups for some experimentation with magnets, for example, was discretely timed as taking just less than one minute to complete.

Liz also occasionally uses a third arrangement when especially large surfaces are required – for instance, for some art activities. This involves the six squares in the group layout moving again to form three long oblongs which, with the static block of four in front of her desk, provides four large surfaces for children to work on (see Figure 3.22).

From the children's viewpoint, there is nothing very unusual or complicated about any of this. It is just how they do things in their classroom – for good and accepted reasons:

... and sometimes when they're in L shapes we work in partners with the person next to us, we don't work in a big group then.

... and we do quite a lot of work in our shapes, most of the time, but when we do, like group work, we move them all together.

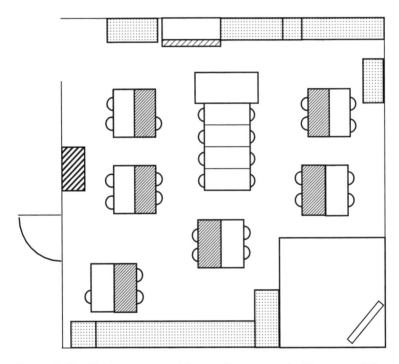

Figure 3.21 Liz's arrangement for small-group work. (Key on p. 56)

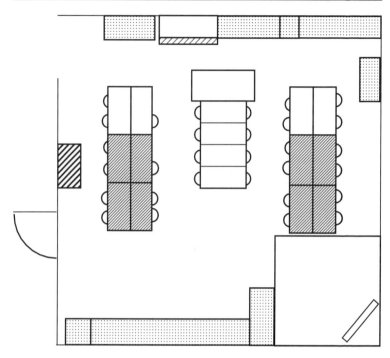

Figure 3.22 Liz's arrangement for large-group work. (Key on p. 56)

Teachers at other schools

Matt Lawrence: Year 6

Matt Lawrence has been teaching at Jesse Boot Primary School in Nottingham for the five years since he completed his PGCE course. He is about to move to a deputy-headship at another city school. During his time at Jesse Boot he has taught across the Key Stage 2 age range and has established a secure reputation among his colleagues, parents and others who visit the school as a well organized, imaginative and highly professional teacher. He frequently hosts student teachers in his class who find him an inspirational and supportive mentor. He is a leading maths teacher.

Matt originally became interested in classroom seating arrangements after reading an article on the subject during his PGCE.

He was struck by the comparison with children handling PE equipment: 'If we can train children to move PE apparatus quickly and easily, then it must be possible to train children to move classroom furniture in a similar way for different activities.'

He felt this was a realistic approach and used the idea as the basis for an education studies presentation during his course. He has continued to develop his ideas since his arrival at the school, adapting to accommodate the physical constraints of the building.

Seen from the road, through the iron railings, Jesse Boot is a pre-war, single-storey building in an elongated 'E' formation, with classrooms leading off a long corridor that stretches the entire length of the school. Part of the school was totally rebuilt following an extensive fire about seven years ago. Some classrooms are square and have a separate glass extension at the rear that acts as a cloakroom and changing room. Others occupy the equivalent floor space and so are larger and rectangular.

The school is situated within Nottingham, at the meeting of two quite different suburbs. One has mostly council housing and also a high level of poverty. The other suburb straddles the city boundary and has some social housing, but also a more substantial proportion of privately owned property. Children from both areas attend and provide the school with a population rich in diversity of peoples, religions and cultures. The nature of the catchment area, as well as the devastating fire and subsequent new buildings, have led the school to develop many strong links with the local community, including use of the premises for a variety of community related purposes.

When Matt first joined the school, he taught a Year 3 class in one of the larger classrooms which allowed plenty of space and flexibility for moving furniture. By using stopwatches and competitive strategies, as well as declaring the class to be a 'magic' class, he enabled the children to become so proficient at moving between arrangements that eventually they could complete the switch in about 25 seconds. He has continued to operate in this way with every class he has led, teaching each about the rationale for having different seating arrangements for different tasks, as well as training them in switching from one to another. While he felt his practice on arrival at the school earned him 'brownie points', initially it meant only the younger children in the school were exposed to moving desks. However, the idea of matching

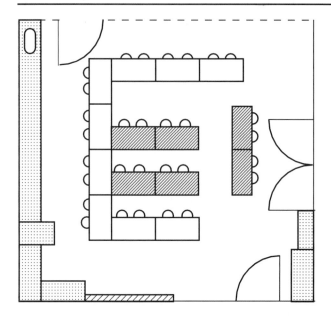

Figure 3.23 Matt's arrangement for individual, paired and whole-class work. (Key on p. 56)

the seating arrangements with the learning objectives became an issue when the whole school was involved in an internal quality assurance exercise. Factors like 'Could all children see the board?' and 'Could they operate in group reading situations?' informed the debate.

Other members of staff knew Matt's practice of moving furniture worked effectively, but it has not been part of any staff development initiative, and while some of his colleagues do now move their furniture, it is not part of any whole school policy.

Matt currently has one of the smaller classrooms for his class of 25 Year 6 children and finds that the limited space available considerably restricts the scope for using varied seating layouts. Nevertheless, he still has two arrangements he uses regularly, as well as tried and tested alternatives for special activities. On some occasions he still cuts up centimetre-square paper to help him plan and think through how the activities and seating will work together: 'I see this as a sort of architectural overview. I have high expectations of my children and believe they can be trained to move furniture easily.'

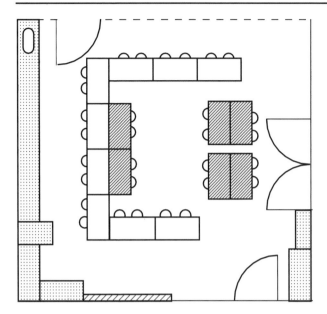

Figure 3.24   Matt's arrangement for small-group work. (Key on p. 56)

The starting point for the arrangements used most regularly is a simple extended 'E' formation (evident in Figure 3.23). The children sit in this pattern for most of the time. It allows free access to resources, easy view of the whiteboard and enables Matt to move around and work with everyone. The second arrangement (see Figure 3.24) involves moving the middle two 'prongs' of the 'E' formation out to the sides of the classroom, to join with other tables. Matt uses the instruction 'Move to a group situation' with the children to move from the 'E' and 'Back to normal' or 'Back to starting position' to return to the 'E' arrangement: 'I don't like rows as I feel it makes the children seem like caged animals. However the current E-shaped formation is probably the best starting option with such a small classroom.'

The small size of the room means that careful thought has had to be given to how the necessary resources are made available without children having to move around too much. For maths sessions, each child starts the 'mental and oral maths' section with an individual 'tool kit' of resources. For English, 'magic' writing boxes or carryalls with dictionaries, an eraser and a sharpener are distributed. One section of the carryall is used for pencil

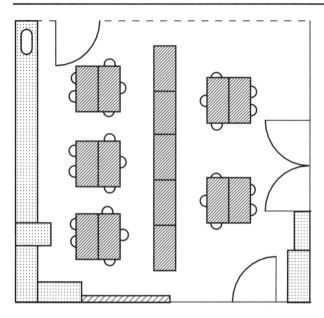

Figure 3.25 Matt's arrangement for special science group work.
(Key on p. 56)

sharpenings so that children don't have to wander out of their seats to the bin.

The furniture moves normally take place about twice a day, often for maths and for topic or science work. Obviously the planning determines the seating, so for a recent science activity requiring access to lots of beakers and apparatus, Matt tried another arrangement. A set of tables was set end-to-end in the centre of the room to hold all the apparatus. On either side of this long table were squares made of two tables, allowing easy access to the equipment (see Figure 3.25).

As well as Matt's own class, other children are also taught in his classroom and so need to be familiar with the different arrangements. The school has three Year 6 classes and sets across the year for maths and English. Matt has the middle target group for maths with 28 children, and a lower attaining English group of about 22 children. As a leading maths teacher he is also responsible for additional maths groups. In addition, on Wednesdays, Thursdays and Fridays, Jackie Flower, the deputy-head, works with the class, specifically with children with English as an additional language. The class has been encouraged to view her as a 'sweeper' (as in a football team) for children who need additional support. For these sessions the seating is altered to the second arrangement (see Figure 3.24) but one of the blocks of eight to ten seats on the right-hand side of the classroom is used for the children working with Jackie. As well as certain named children, anyone in the class can choose to work with her if they feel they are having difficulties. There is no stigma attached to working with Jackie. Children choose to sit around her and will move out of the way and sit in any spare seat when they feel they can manage on their own. The arrangement works well.

Jackie, a teacher with many years experience, feels the different seating arrangements are effective because they enable children to work well and to support one another.

Moving between arrangements does not take long as not all of the classroom furniture is moved. Any image of seats being passed over desks this way and that would be unrealistic. Most of the desks stay where they are, while some are rotated. Jackie suggests that the simplicity of the change is one of the great merits of the approach that Matt has developed in this classroom where space is at a premium: 'I feel moving the desks is just one piece of the jigsaw to the learning environment, and the children are beginning to put the pieces together for themselves.'

Matt actively promotes children's self-assessment, and not only with the choice to work with Jackie. He also gets them to score their own involvement and performance in groups. When the children are working in the group arrangement, most commonly for topic work or science, he initially scores each group out of ten and then, every 15 minutes, they have to score themselves. He believes that this approach 'Helps children to learn how to cope with each other and how to work in groups and have a genuine feel for the "team".'

He has these expectations of all children that come into his classroom, not just his own class. A good example of this is when Matt's own class exchanges with another Year 6 class of 26 children. Most of them have been taught by Matt for their maths or English target groups or when they were in Year 3, so when he asks them to move into 'a group situation' they know what needs to happen. Again, only the children on the middle 'prongs' of the 'E' move their tables and chairs to the side to form the familiar Figure 3.24 arrangement and even with this class the move still only takes a minute.

How the grouped arrangement works in practice can be demonstrated in a science revision session for the SATs. Matt allows children to choose to sit in friendship groups of four. Using his knowledge of the children's interests, he encourages them to use their favourite cartoon characters to aid their revision on 'Light'. Each group is expected to produce one A3-sized diagram or drawing to illustrate some aspect of 'Light' that the whole class can then use for revision. The groups choose to operate in different ways with some allocating parts of the task to individuals or pairs and then sharing ideas before creating the diagram. Other groups operate as teams with everyone involved in every part of the task as they go along.

Even when seated in groups there is little flexibility for movement around the classroom, so the children stay in their seats and put their hands up with queries. Consequently Matt has to move around a great deal to give individuals and groups encouragement. One child near the front needs extra help to see objects or text as he is visually impaired. Matt makes a special trip towards him to show what he has just shown to the rest of class, as he needs to be about 15cm away from the child's face in order for the child to see clearly. The level of on-task engagement throughout the activity is good, and the move back to the starting 'E' arrangement is smooth and conducted without fuss.

Matt's architectural overview, evident in his planning, coupled with high expectations of his children and his simple training techniques have resulted in a strategy that children can remember and operate easily, and that can be adapted to fit any shape and size of classroom.

Melanie Tatley: Reception and Year 1

Melanie Tatley is the deputy-head at St Peter's Church of England Primary School in the attractive commuter village of East Bridgford about ten miles to the east of Nottingham. She has taught here since 1998 and currently has a Year 1 class.

Melanie began experimenting with seating arrangements in her previous school when she had a 'lively' Year 3/4 class. As part of a project on 'The Victorians' she rearranged the furniture into rows so that the children could try working as their great-grandparents might have done in their schooldays. She soon began to notice that her children responded to this unfamiliar environment in ways she had not anticipated. In both class teaching and individual work, children were less distracted and concentration was better than usual. Struck by the difference that this change made, she continued using row arrangements for some activities beyond the end of the project and found that the effects endured.

A few years later she heard a talk on the issue and decided to try using varied arrangements with a younger age group. She has now been operating in this way in her current classroom for the last two years. As Melanie teaches Reception and Year 1 children, her class grows in size throughout the academic year as children reach their 5th birthday and start school.

She is aware that some other teachers in her present school have used her approach, and the school's headteacher has undertaken observations in Melanie's class and been both interested and impressed by what he saw. An LEA adviser has also observed her practice and was similarly interested. Indeed, it was from him that we first learned of Melanie's use of flexible seating arrangements. The school's policy is to encourage teachers to use their classroom in the manner that they find best matches their purposes and the space and resources available, and this is certainly what Melanie does.

The school as a whole is housed in two separate buildings. To the rear of the plot is a 1960s single storey, flat roofed, half-timber and glass building, where the Key Stage 2 classes are based. To the front, nearer the road and main entrance, and in the centre of the playground, is the other part of the school – a high-gabled, Victorian stone structure which is home for the school's two Key Stage 1 classrooms. This was the original school building and is typical of many village schools in the region, built in the late nineteenth century when education in school became a legal requirement. Nowadays, the school's catchment area extends well beyond the original village, which has grown with both private and council housing. In the recent past, it also included children from service families based at a nearby RAF station who were bussed between their homes on the camp and the school.

Melanie's classroom is entered through a short passageway from the main entrance to the old school. Also leading off from this passageway is a small meeting room with a kitchen, the

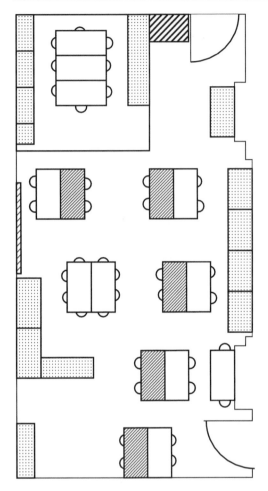

Figure 3.26 Melanie's arrangement for small-group work. (Key on p. 56)

children's cloakroom and a large open area. This area is shared by both the Key Stage 1 classes and has a variety of uses. For instance, when the school's LSAs or other helpers and parents work with small groups they can take them here from their class. The area is also used for some whole-class activities involving audio-visual equipment and for drama. The two classrooms are reasonably spacious, rectangular in shape and separated by a floor-to-ceiling, wood and glass, folding partition. A few years back, when team teaching operated, the partition was folded back to allow easy access between the classrooms. Now, however, the two classes operate more independently and the partition is treated as the back wall of each classroom, opposite the whiteboards, and forms part of a display area behind some storage trolleys.

Melanie's classroom furniture is a set of standard rectangular tables of the kind found in most classrooms, and chairs with moulded plastic seats, all of an appropriately small size for this Year 1 and Reception class. She has developed three basic arrangements for her classroom, each associated with a working style that she identifies by name with the children. For 'group work' the children sit in groups of mostly four to six, around two tables drawn together to form a square surface (see Figure 3.26). For 'large group work', for example in technology, art or sometimes maths, when large surfaces are required, children can be seated in groups of up to 12, around four tables (see Figure 3.27). An interesting and unusual feature of the large group work layout is that, even when seated like this, no one has their back to the whiteboard, as children sit at only three sides of the working surface. This means that both arrangements can support not only group work or work requiring plenty of space, but also, and as effectively, whole-class teaching.

The third arrangement is for what Melanie and her class refer to as 'quiet work' (see Figure 3.28). When the task is for each child to be working on their own or when pairs are to collaborate, but quietly, children sit in twos at single tables, spaced out in columns, and all facing the whiteboard. Although the desks in each line stand separately, this formation could be reasonably described as 'rows', but it is not. By calling it the 'quiet work' layout instead, the nature of the work and behaviour that it supports is immediately and consistently evident. It also avoids triggering the negative connotations that 'rows' has for some adults.

Being based in a relatively spacious Victorian classroom, originally designed to accommodate many more children than it does today, means there is sufficient space for the current class of 29 children to have seating arrangements which vary, without disturbing either the separate carpet area or the three dedicated art tables. However, this situation does alter as the year progresses and the class numbers grow:

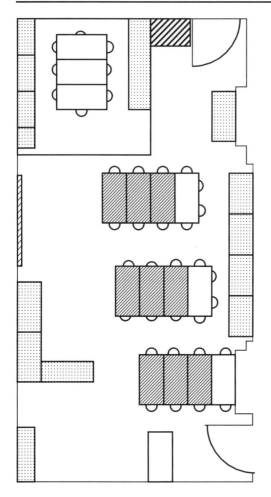

Figure 3.27   Melanie's arrangement for large-group work. (Key on p. 56)

I operated a flexible approach last year, but when the class grew to 34 there simply wasn't enough room to have all the children seated in pairs. So instead, I kept some children seated in group formations during their paired or individual work but rotated everyone to ensure they all had the chance to operate in different arrangements.

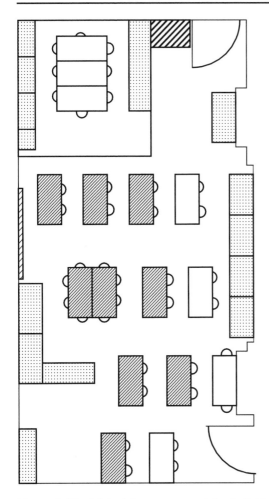

Figure 3.28 Melanie's arrangement for individual, paired and whole-class work (quiet work). (Key on p. 56)

As the children are so young and also relatively inexperienced in the ways of school, Melanie feels it is important at the beginning of the year to spend some time ensuring that all the children are able to move furniture safely and can appropriately organize the classroom. In practice, this time spent in training the children is surprisingly short, yet in Melanie's experience it reaps long-term benefits in terms of time saved throughout the year:

At the beginning of the year, training the children to move the furniture into the various arrangements takes about half an hour. After this they can usually move between the different arrangements in just under a minute. Most of the children are involved, and they either push or pull their own table into position in their pairs. I generally let them choose their own partners in order to sit in pairs. Occasionally, I sort out the pairings but I've found the children tend to choose partners of similar attainment levels anyway. I ask them to choose a new partner each half-term, so across the year most of them will have worked with six other children in the paired arrangement.

Moving between the three layouts happens about two or three times a day. As the day begins on the carpet and moves into 'quiet work', the first move is usually to rearrange the tables from the 'group work' setting that they were left in at the end of the previous day. The 'group work' configuration is used for about 70 per cent of literacy sessions and also for many sessions in other subjects. However, the 'quiet work' paired arrangement is used a great deal for numeracy and for extended writing. Overall, the 'quiet work' arrangement is used a good deal less frequently than the 'group work' setting. However, the difference and the move between the two does act as a clear signal for the children about the nature of the work that they are undertaking and about the kinds of behaviour that are appropriate to that task and setting:

> Initially, I wasn't certain that using flexible seating arrangements would be appropriate with such young children, so I tried it for some activities last year and I was very impressed by the children's attention and progress, particularly in writing using the 'quiet work' arrangement. The progress in the first two weeks of the year was dramatic: I couldn't believe it. They were on task 70–80 per cent more and their work was at least 70–80 per cent better in quality.

On intake in September 1999, at least 25 per cent of the children in Melanie's class entered school with little or no knowledge of their letters. However, informal teacher assessment of all the children, completed after seven months in the class, showed all of them having a reading age above their chronological age, with some children as many as five years in advance. In addition, many children were writing one or two sides of A4 without help: 'I would put this achievement down to how the children get on during "quiet work". I also feel that this year's class is in advance of last year's class because I'm using flexible seating arrangements all the time now.'

Melanie has recently completed her National Professional Quali-fication for Headship (NPQH) training and is currently applying for headships. When asked about how, as a headteacher, she might want to develop a whole-school approach, she had little doubt:

> I'd want to promote a flexible approach to seating arrangements in any school I led, but I realize it would have to be introduced sensitively and I'd need to offer a great deal of encouragement. The advantage is that I can demonstrate from my own experience and practice that using a flexible approach does make a difference to children's learning.

Carol Edmunds: Years 1 and 2

Carol Edmunds is an experienced teacher who works at St Mary's, a large voluntary controlled primary school. The school is situ-ated on a main thoroughfare through Bulwell, one of the former villages that now forms part of the city of Nottingham. St Mary's is one of eight primary and two secondary schools in the Not-tingham (Bulwell) Education Action Zone (EAZ).

Unlike other teachers whose practices are described in these pages, Carol only recently changed her classroom layout, as a con-sequence of participating in an EAZ initiative. She was one among a group of teachers from EAZ schools to explore the potential of using classroom organization strategically to enhance children's learning. This experience led her to develop her thoughts on creating environments to support her children's attention and, so she hoped, improve their learning and attainment.

Like a good number of schools, St Mary's consists of two buildings on either side of a playground. The taller and older of the
two backs onto the road, is built of the familiar sandstone of the
locality and dates back to the Victorian era. It currently houses
the Key Stage 1 classes. The other, a single storey, half-glass,
half-brick building, was constructed in the 1960s and accommod-
ates the Key Stage 2 classes, the hall, dining room and nursery.

As its inclusion in an EAZ might suggest, St Mary's is one of a
number of schools serving an area that scores high on a number
of indicators of disadvantage. Educational attainment has been
well below national averages at all stages, as has progression to
post-16 education. Attendance rates at the local secondary schools
have caused concern, and teenage pregnancy and unemployment levels run well above national norms.

Since the EAZ's inception in 1999, and with substantial support
from the new city LEA, the EAZ primary schools have made
remarkable progress, with Bulwell St. Mary's among those making
the most rapid and substantial gains. Using Key Stage 2 results as
an indicator, the percentage of the school's Year 6 children achieving Level 4+ has risen from 49 per cent in 1998 to 82 per cent in
2000 for English. For mathematics, the improvement over the
same period was from 32 to 62 per cent and for science from 24
to 97 per cent. Even against rising national figures, these are
substantial gains. Ofsted inspected the school late in 1999, found
teaching to be satisfactory or better in 94 per cent of observed
lessons and commended as 'excellent' the leadership provided
by the then newly appointed headteacher, Phil Ball. Indeed, following publication of the 2000 Key Stage 2 results, St Mary's was
publicly acclaimed for being among the most improved primary
schools in England.

Carol's initiative and innovations in her classroom practice
therefore took place in the context of substantial encouragement
for development and commitment to providing stimulating and
effective teaching. Her classroom runs the width of the older of
the school's buildings and was formerly the school's hall. It was
converted into a classroom in 1998.

Her normal practice had been to group her mixed Year 1 and
Year 2 class into four 'bases', each consisting of six children who
sat together around grouped tables. Although the room was spacious, this arrangement meant that some children still sat with

their backs to the board, which proved problematic during whole-class teaching (see Figure 3.29). When first considering how to improve her children's attention and progress, Carol wanted to ensure that everyone could see the board easily, but she also wanted to keep a friendly feel in the room by preserving some semblance of the 'bases': 'I was very sceptical to start with [about changed classroom layouts], but I managed not to lose the group work and group identity as I could always move the desks. The children just pulled the desks apart at the end of a group work session.'

She opted to separate each set of three tables (the original 'bases') to create an exploded 'U' shape. The tables, with two children sitting at each, were arranged in small horseshoes, but without joining together (see Figure 3.30). In this arrangement, used primarily for individual or paired work, all of the children were able to see the board easily and, by keeping a 'U' shape, the sense of belonging to bases was retained. For group work the sets of three tables were pushed back together.

The resulting improvements in children's involvement with their work were so marked that Carol rechecked the observational data gathered by her assistant, only to conclude that they were correct. The observations focused on a sample of six children and took place during the 20-minute period of 'group and independent work' within the Literacy Hour. They showed an overall 'on-task' level of 71 per cent for the whole group for the first week, with the daily rates ranging from 61 to 83 per cent. The overall level for the second week was 91 per cent, with the daily rates ranging from 84 to 100 per cent.

In addition to the overall picture, the observational evidence highlighted one child, thought to be a chatterbox, who turned out to have the best 'on-task' scores: 'For me, the greatest effect was on the children who had been the most distracted.' As for the school's response, Carol commented:

Another teacher in the school came and had a look and then went back and changed his classroom in a similar way. And in terms of looking at other areas, apart from our own classrooms, it has made all the staff talk about how they organize space and has opened up the discussion on these issues.

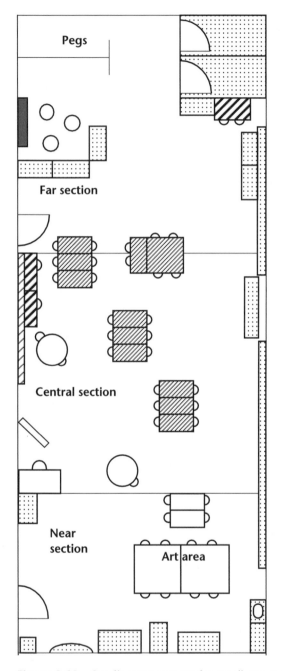

Figure 3.29 Carol's arrangement for small-group work (1999). (Key on p. 56)

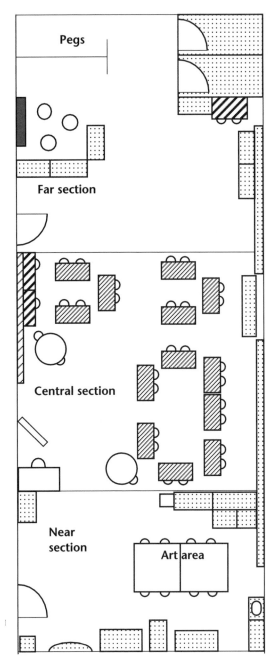

Figure 3.30 Carol's arrangement for individual, paired and whole-class work (1999). (Key on p. 56)

The class as a whole seemed to like the arrangements, although Carol felt at the time that there were still issues relating to resources that she needed to address:

> In practical terms, the changes were problematic as I had only moved the desks around. It revealed the issue of glue, pencil pots and other resources. You need to give each child access, if they're working in pairs on desks. Because of where the resources are placed in the room, everyone had to weave in and out of the tables to get at apparatus and trays. However, children actually complained about being disturbed. When asked if they wanted the desks changing back the children said, 'No, don't change it back as it makes us work harder'. I thought this could just be the children giving me the answers I wanted to hear, but I listened in on some conversations between children, which did confirm their earlier comments.

A year on from changing her classroom layout, and still teaching in the same classroom, Carol now has 23 Year 2 children in her class. She developed her approach further and now organises her classroom in three main areas. You enter the room at one end, nearest to the permanent art area with the sink and large tables. The central part of the classroom is carpeted and it is here that children sit and work for most of their activities. This is the area where most of the changes to seating arrangements happen. At the far end, there is room for coats and a quiet reading area, as well as new cupboards and one of the computer stations.

Carol's concerns about the location of and access to the resources in the arrangement she operated in the previous year have been addressed in her arrangements for this year's class. Trays and other shared resources are now distributed evenly around the room, ensuring easier, closer access for all children. The tables are now mostly formed into L-shapes rather than the exploded-U-shapes (with one exception – see Figure 3.31) and each set of two tables has a cup of wax crayons and a 'desk tidy', containing sharp pencils and other essential stationery, such as sharpeners and erasers.

Some of the children, now Year 2, were in Carol's class last year and have had two years to get used to moving furniture for

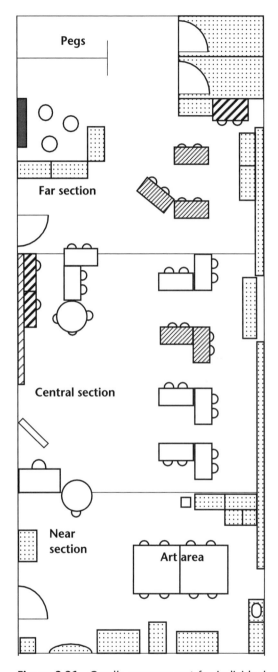

Figure 3.31 Carol's arrangement for individual, paired and whole-class work (2000). (Key on p. 56)

different activities. The fluency with which changes are made was well illustrated during an observed session. Carol has all the children on the open carpet area for the Literacy Hour. Each child is a member of a group for the allocation of work (Kipper, Biff, Chips and Floppy). For the group and independent work section of the Literacy Hour, Carol distributes and explains the task for each group and, within a minute of her dismissing the children from the carpet, they are all sitting down working.

In this brief period, and with minimal fuss, two of the four groups alter their tables, moving from L-shapes to a square or, in the case of the three-tabled group, to a rectangle, to suit the work they are about to do. The striking thing for an observer is that at no time in the previous few minutes did Carol give any instruction about altering the seating arrangements. The fact that the changes were so slight, so effortlessly made and were not initiated by the teacher accounted for them being nearly missed during the observation.

The children were given a task to complete and, having completely understood and internalized the benefits of creating an environment to support an activity, took it on themselves to move their furniture to create a suitable working environment (see Figure 3.32). When asked about this, Carol laughs: 'Actually they're slipping today, because often the group I'm working with go and get the big red chair for me to sit on as well!' She adds:

> I believe in giving children independence to make
> decisions for themselves. They know they can change the
> furniture around, and that the expectation is that they
> should match the seating to the task purpose. Because
> they know that's what I expect, they feel confident they
> can make those decisions.

Throughout the rest of this session, there is a general quiet buzz of talk and purposeful activity. Two of the groups are either involved with Carol or in playing a game. For the remaining two groups the activities seem to determine the amount and type of talk involved. One has the task of matching sets of questions and answers and is busy in animated, though not too noisy, debate. The other group is gathered in the art area where each member has the task of drawing the weeping fig plant. Although

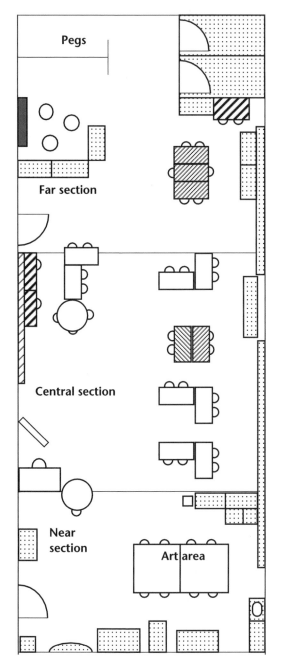

Far section

Pegs

Central section

Near
section

Art area

Figure 3.32 Carol's arrangement for small-group work (2000).
(Key on p. 56)

this is not a collaborative or cooperative task, as everyone has to do their own drawing, some of their conversation is about their art work.

At the end of the session, children who had altered their tables a little earlier quickly and quietly swivel them back to the starting arrangement, again without any instruction, and clearly demonstrate the confidence in making their own decisions about their working space that Carol is trying to promote with her flexible approach to seating arrangements.

Part 3
Turning the tables?

4 Please take your seats!

Children in the classes and schools described in the preceding pages have a different experience of classroom life from most of their peers in neighbouring schools and classrooms. At present, we lack systematic evidence of the additional benefits that they might derive from working in classrooms that change to suit the tasks, but their teachers are in no doubt that the strategies they have developed enable them to teach more effectively and their pupils to gain more from school. The benefits these teachers have identified in conversations with us are not restricted to improvements in attention, progress and classroom behaviour, important though these are. Several teachers also highlighted how rearranging the classroom for different types of activity has prompted a greater level of awareness among children of these different learning activities, of their purposes and of the kinds of interaction and attention that each entails. In other words, children's understanding of classroom learning and of the differences between learning activities, signalled by the reconfiguration of furniture, seems to improve. Although this might appear to be a rather sophisticated metacognitive development, Melanie Tatley also noted it with her Reception and Year 1 children. A further, but related, benefit reported by some teachers is that the activity of changing the classroom layout adds another dimension of structure to a day's activities. Children's classroom experience comes to be differentiated not only by the curriculum but also by context: their days seem to become more varied.

It is not only for their children that teachers have found a strategic seating approach worthwhile. Several told how the gains they saw in children's work and learning increased their own confidence and satisfaction as teachers, which no doubt, in turn, additionally benefits their pupils. Many also expressed the feeling, in one way or another, of being more aware of how the whole class, and every individual, is feeling and progressing and, consequently, of feeling more 'on top of things'. It is, of course, not surprising that these teachers value the pedagogical approaches they have developed: if they did not, they would not work as they do. However, while the benefits they describe are important to record, we must again emphasize that, as yet, the evidence of these beneficial outcomes has to be regarded as anecdotal and subjective. This is not to diminish the potential value or validity of these insights; it is simply to note that systematic evaluation of the consequences of strategic seating has not yet been undertaken. In the meantime, however, schools are full of children, so teachers have to make judgements and decisions on the basis of their beliefs, experience and imagination, informed by existing research evidence, albeit incomplete.

In Part 1 of this book we developed the argument that the common practice of arranging primary classrooms in groups, irrespective of the work children are asked to do, warrants reconsideration. Practice will not develop to incorporate the implications of all the evidence and arguments reviewed in Part 1 unless teachers become persuaded, individually and collectively, that there are viable and acceptable alternatives to established practice which can benefit learning. The purpose of Part 2 was to provide examples of primary teachers who create working environments that support the variety of learning activities they provide for their pupils and to describe their experience of working in this way. It is important that we reiterate that these cases are not intended to be models for imitation, although we hope they will inspire and be a fruitful source of ideas. They simply describe the practices and experiences of real teachers and pupils in real classrooms facing all the same issues, challenges and constraints as other English primary schools early in the twenty-first century.

If Part 1 has persuaded you that the ubiquitous practice of group seating creates unnecessary difficulties for children and their teachers, and if Part 2 has left you thinking that the idea of varying classroom organization to match the demands of learning activities is not just theoretically sensible but also practically viable, the rest of Part 3 should be of interest to you. We have planned it as a resource for teachers who want to 'have a go'. The intention is not to provide the equivalent of a self-assembly flatpack with step-by-step instructions, so much as a tool kit of ideas and strategies from which you can select those that might be useful for your situation.

The starting points for any change in practice tend to be experiences, events or ideas that prompt questions about that practice. For many of the teachers we have spoken to, these have been articles in the educational press, conversations with other teachers or seeing another teacher vary their classroom organization strategically. In Matt Lawrence's case, for example, his initial awareness of the research evidence came from reading about it in the educational press. Melanie, however, changed her classroom layout for curriculum reasons, to focus on 'The Victorians', but noticed marked differences in the ways that children worked and in their progress. Lesley Beaton, who entered teaching having already established a successful career in the financial sector, varied her classroom from the outset simply because it seemed 'obvious'. Each simply 'had a go' and arrived at their current practice by trial and error over a period of time. For others, the experience was less solitary – as when whole schools or key stage teams looked at the ideas and implemented changes together.

Although we suggest below a sequence of steps that might prove helpful, the end can be reached by any number of different routes. We have organized these steps and the tools within this tool kit into the familiar stages of review, planning, implementation and evaluation, but these suggestions exist only to be pillaged for all you can find that serves your, or your school's, purposes and needs.

Reviewing your current practice

Whatever your current practice, it will have merits and these need to be noted. However, if you want to try out some new ideas, it will probably be because your current arrangements produce some outcomes that you want to improve: these are worth identifying with some clarity. You may also want to note aspects of practice that you are not prepared to sacrifice to get those improvements. Listed below are suggestions and tools to support your thinking in this stage, ranging from those that can best be done in an armchair to others that entail a little more activity.

Reflection

Whatever else you do, you will certainly need to 'have a think' about your classroom and the way it works at present. Indeed, if you have got this far, you have almost certainly already begun to do so. Reflection is not a navel-gazing exercise: it can also usefully draw on ideas and evidence taken from your context as well as from elsewhere. To support your reflection and assessment of how things work at present in your classroom, or in any other in which you have an interest or responsibilities, here are some general questions to begin your consideration.

- Why was your classroom originally organized like this? Were there good reasons? Do those reasons still apply?
- What are the main features of the present layout that you value, and why?
- Are there difficult areas within the classroom, in relation to access to resources or because they have heavy pedestrian traffic, for instance?
- What are the main types of work that you expect your pupils to undertake when seated at their places? (Consider the five types of learning activity described in Chapter 1.) Do the seating arrangements support these tasks equally well? Which work well and which less well?
- Think of the children whose attention and/or behaviour cause you most concern. Could their seating and working positions contribute to their difficulties? (You might try taking a child's-eye view by sitting in a few places to see what the classroom world looks like from their perspective.)

• What are the main aspects of children's attention, work involvement and behaviour that you would like to improve? Is the need for improvement evident during all five types of learning activity?

Mapping

Taking a good look at a familiar landscape can be difficult and, as full-time primary teachers generally spend in excess of 1000 hours in their classrooms each year, they will know them better than their own front rooms. To be able to take a good look at the well known, it has to be rendered a little strange and unfamiliar. The simplest way of doing this is to sketch a plan view of the classroom or working area, as in the figures presented in Part 2, showing where the desks, board, cupboards, computers and other resources are currently located, as well as pupils' seating positions. Initially the sketches can be rough, but scale drawings may be useful at a later stage when thinking about other possible layouts.

Eliciting views

Conversations with children about their classrooms can be goldmines of insight. The opportunity to suggest improvements, unconstrained by budget, does not only produce fanciful and fantastic ideas, it often identifies aspects of current classroom life where frustrations arise. In our experience, children understand the distinction between classroom environments in which they work well and those that they enjoy for other reasons. They also recognize that different tasks make different demands. Many of our case study teachers have found the involvement of the children at this stage to be beneficial to the whole process of changing the environment. First, the children have a unique perspective in terms of their learning experiences and from their physical viewpoint. Second, this involvement engages children's interest and enables them to 'own' some of the developments that may come about.

It is not only children's perspectives and experiences that can inform review and reflection, however. LSAs who regularly work in a classroom are often better placed to see how things work from the children's point of view than their teacher: they may also be better able to articulate their observations and suggestions than younger children. Moreover, classroom layouts need to support LSAs' own work as well children's learning. Headteachers and other regular visitors to classrooms may also have useful observations to make.

Assessing the match between learning activities and settings

The key point of this whole book is that classroom organization should support the requirements of learning activities. We suggested in Chapter 1 that learning activities can usefully be thought of as falling into five categories. Children are asked to work with their teacher, as individuals, in groups or as a whole class, or to work alone or in collaboration without their teacher. Part of the process of reviewing current practice is taking a view of the degree of match provided by current arrangements. This can be done just through reflection or by using more systematic evidence.

The informal approach is to estimate how a normal week's routine will distribute the demands on children's classroom time between the five types of activity. The cautionary note we would sound is that it is easy to overestimate the time attributed to some of the less common activities. A more accurate assessment will arise from using one or two weeks' detailed teaching plans and by focusing on what this would mean for a few individual children. Time spent on activities outside the classroom, for PE for instance, should be ignored. However you do it, this assessment should result in your estimate of how children's time in the class is distributed between the different types of activity.

The question then is whether the seating arrangements provide a good enough match for the activities. If not, which types are well supported and which do not appear to be?

A further approach to assessing the level of match provided is to undertake an assessment using direct observation. The 'Checking for Match' grid (see Figure 4.1) is a simple device for recording the extent of match between seating arrangements and tasks. The categories along each side can be adapted to suit the situation and purpose, as the example shown illustrates by distinguishing between pairs and groups for both seating arrangements

Task working . . .

	On own	As a pair	In a group	As a class
As a class				
With others				
As a pair			▓▓▓▓	
On own			▓▓▓▓	

Seating . . .

Figure 4.1 'Checking for Match' grid

and learning activities. The grid can be completed by the class teacher, an LSA or another adult who notes the work that a chosen child *is meant to be doing* and the context in which they are to undertake that work, and then enters a tick in the appropriate box on the grid. Then another child is observed and the process is repeated. With a schedule such as this, there is little to be gained by having an interval of less than about 15 minutes between observations but, over the course of a few days, the grid will begin to yield a pattern that can inform reflection. The two cells shaded on the grid are those in which ticks suggesting a mismatch most commonly fall.

Recording 'on-task' levels

Most of the case studies reviewed in Chapter 2 assessed the impact of different seating arrangements on children's attention to their individual work, defined as time on-task. The easiest way to monitor children's activity in the classroom is to use an observation schedule with just two categories of behaviour: 'on-task' and 'off-task'. 'On-task' means that the child is doing what they are meant to be doing. This can include getting resources, discussing a point with a neighbour or waiting for the teacher, as well as clearly 'working', depending on the task in hand. Chatting, daydreaming or fiddling with a shoe would count as 'off-task'.

10-second periods	Child 1	Child 2	Child 3	Child 4
1				
2				
3				
4				
5				
6				
7				
8				
9				
10				
Total on-task				
% on-task				

Figure 4.2   An observation schedule for recording on-task and off-task behaviour

What constitutes 'daydreaming' is probably one of the hardest aspects to define, at least in principle. Generally, however, teachers have little difficulty in determining whether the child is gazing out of the window lost in a dream about the latest Harry Potter story or deciding how best to complete the task in hand. Often, watching for a few further seconds establishes the 'on' or 'off' nature of the daydream.

The observation schedule shown in Figure 4.2 can be used to record up to four children simultaneously. The four can be selected because of their individual qualities or simply to function as 'barometers' for the whole class. The observer has to be able to sit, watch and record, so a class teacher normally needs to enlist some help. The procedure is to observe Child 1 for 10 seconds and, if they are on-task for all that period, place a tick in Row 1. If they are off-task, a cross is inserted. Attention then moves to Child 2 for whom the process is repeated. When all the children under observation have been sampled once, the observer focuses again on Child 1 and records a tick or cross for Period 2 in the second box under 'Child 1'. At the end of the observation, time on-task for each child can be computed by dividing the number of ticks by the number of observations and multiplying by 100. As an example, a child observed to be working for 6 of 12 10-second periods will have been on-task for 50 per cent of observed time. However, it is important to repeat this type of exercise for half and hour or so on several different days, as patterns of behaviour vary a good deal from day to day and task by task.

Recording average on-task levels can yield useful insights into how children actually spend their time in the classroom, but the resulting figures can also be valuable as a baseline against which to assess any improvements arising from trials of new seating arrangements. This was how the measure was used in many of the studies mentioned in Chapter 2.

Planning for change

However you have gone about it, the process of reviewing what you, and possibly your colleagues, currently do will have generated ideas about areas in which you want to secure improvement. It may also have spawned thoughts about how new classroom organization strategies might bring these about. However, before introducing any changes to classroom routines, it is advisable to take a while to plan how all this is to happen. In this section, suggestions are offered for planning change in one classroom and also for when classroom organization is to be the focus for a whole staff or team.

Planning for change in your own classroom

For a teacher thinking of developing a strategic approach to classroom organization, decisions have to be made about the new layouts themselves and about how the shift from one arrangement to another will be made. We suggest starting by identifying which of the five types of learning activity are most frequent in your pupils' experience. In most classrooms, this turns out to be individual work, followed by whole-class teaching, with collaborative work running third. Whichever it is, sketch some possible layouts that could 'fit' and support this type of activity. The size and shape of the room will constrain the possibilities, as will the number of children, but most classrooms allow for some of the horseshoes, exploded-U, U-, T-, L- or E-shaped arrangements described in Part 2 to be used. For areas shared with other teachers, designated quiet areas or discussion tables may be possible. You will need to draw a more detailed plan of your preferred layout, including computer table, cupboards, etc. If your plan is for individual or 'quiet' work, how could it easily be reconfigured to support group work? Work out the minimum number of table and chair moves. When you have a possible 'solution', try a dry run at the end of the school day! Enlisting the help of a colleague is invaluable in this process, not only to help with the furniture moving itself but also for talking over the possibilities.

When you have settled on your classroom layouts, and assuming there is more than one, the detailed planning of which pieces of furniture are to move and who is to move them needs attention. Maps and cut-out shapes representing tables and chairs can be helpful in sorting out exactly which pieces of furniture are to move. You will need to make sure at this point that any moving of furniture can be done in accordance with normal health and safety policy and practice. You also need to decide whether moving the furniture is to be done by all children or whether you are to have a small designated 'removals team', membership of which might change on a weekly or fortnightly basis. Whatever approach you settle on, there will have to be a training phase in which the children are briefed about the new arrangement and its rationale, and practise the actual business of transforming the classroom from one layout to another – safely, quietly and quickly. This will take half an hour or so but the investment of training time at this stage will save delays and confusion later: transitions should be completed in around 60 seconds.

Your planning may also need to take into account the legitimate interests of others. LSAs and others who regularly work in your classroom will need to know your plans and may well be involved in shaping them. Thought should also be given to briefing colleagues, including your headteacher. Parents will notice and be interested as soon as changes are evident: if they are not to be told beforehand, you need to be ready to offer a clear account of why you are trying a new approach, without suggesting that you are 'experimenting' with their children. Introducing a change such as this at one of the natural breaks in the school year minimizes disruption and concern. We suggest that you plan to begin at the start of a term or after a half-term break.

Planning for change across a team or whole school

If you are a headteacher or team leader and are persuaded that the approaches outlined earlier should be developed in your school, your planning will include a staff development programme to brief and engage your staff, many of whom will be unfamiliar with the ideas and information that have interested you. For the initiative-weary, another new idea may also be unwelcome.

Two of the possible approaches to engaging a staff team in strategic classroom management are to introduce the whole team to the ideas through a staff development programme or, before doing this, for one teacher to try the approach in just one classroom. A 'one-classroom, in-house pilot' raises general awareness of the idea and provides local first-hand, and therefore highly credible, experience to inform the later whole-school or team development programme. Whatever the chosen approach, planning has to include briefing on the research evidence, opportunities to discuss the possible merits of a more strategic approach to classroom organization, time to review and note the strengths of current practice and the chance to shift some furniture around in the school's teaching areas. In working with schools on INSET days, we have found a viable pattern for training to be a presentation and open discussion of the issues and evidence described in Part 1, followed by brainstorming on possible alternative ways of working and illustration of a few of the cases from Part 2 or, even better, a brief presentation by someone who has tried to improve the match between organization and learning activities in their own teaching. Cases available on the classroom organization website at http://education.ntu.ac.uk/research/primaryclassorg could be drawn on for these purposes. Teachers encountering the idea of changing classroom layouts several times a week for the first time will express reservations, many of them entirely reasonable, about the time taken to moving furniture, safety issues and the constraints of space and furniture design. Reservations may also be expressed about the reactions of parents and Ofsted: these all need to be aired and discussed.

Exploring these ideas in discussion is one thing, but they only come to life when the furniture moves. The most productive exercise, in our experience, is for time to be allocated to allow teachers to move from the presentation and discussion session into classrooms and, in teams of three or four, to look at each classroom, consider its current layout and then try different arrangements. Often there are natural groupings of teachers arising from the structure of the school, such as the team teaching three Year 3/4 classes. Discussions in these small teams often raise questions not only about the arrangement of children's tables and chairs but also about the function or location of other furniture, including more fixed items such as wall-mounted whiteboards.

Sessions like these need to be followed up and, if change is to be implemented across a school, it really has to be planned! Plans will also generally cover arrangements for supporting teachers trying new strategies and for addressing the inevitably differing levels of enthusiasm, interest and success in finding worthwhile alternatives. As with all staff development programmes, this cannot all be brought about through one training session or INSET day: follow-up sessions for discussion of what has and has not proved fruitful will be needed. If, as a consequence of all the discussions, change is to be comprehensive and to affect several or all classes, governors and parents will probably need to be informed in advance.

Implementation

Planning is one thing: doing it, as they say, is another. The initial stage of implementation will be difficult as it will involve new ways of working for everyone. For teachers, the first few days are more than normally tiring. Until the new routines and procedures settle down, children will need more careful monitoring and prompting, which place additional demands on teachers' attention and energy. Outside the classroom too, teachers' work on short- and medium-term planning will now have to include the new considerations of seating arrangements and scheduling the points when furniture, children or both are to move.

Any new arrangement will give rise to unforeseen difficulties and frustrations, as well as, hopefully, some of the planned benefits. The temptation to abandon the innovation within a few days may be strong if expectations are not all immediately fulfilled. However, precisely because new routines take time to become habitual and established, this temptation should be resisted for at least a couple of weeks if at all possible. Where problems arise, plans can be revised to try to get around them. Most important of all, interest and support from colleagues can be crucial: changing your own well-established practices is never easy.

Evaluation

Any changes that you or your colleagues implement will have been with a view to bringing about improvements in important aspects of classroom processes or learning outcomes. There comes a point at which it is sensible to ask whether the improvements that these changes were designed to produce have materialized and, if they have, whether they have been sufficient to offset any costs or losses that also seem to have been incurred. Evaluation is a process of assessing relative values – it is not a process of measurement, but evidence can inform those judgements of value. If evidence has been collected before, possibly throughout the period of changed practice, and again when it has been in operation for a while, perhaps using tools introduced earlier in this chapter, aspects of the extent of improvement can be assessed. If children were asked at an earlier stage, they can be asked again about the new ways of working and what they make of them; they may also shed light on why, for instance, off-task levels have changed. In the end, however, drawing on as many sources or evidence as might be relevant and available, it will be the class teacher's assessment that must determine whether a better working environment for supporting learning and teaching has been developed in each classroom.

If you develop your approach to classroom organization, whether as a teacher working alone or as a member of a team, and establish a strategic approach to seating in your classroom or school that you would be prepared to share with other teachers, please contact us through the primary classroom organization website (http://education.ntu.ac.uk/research/primaryclassorg) to see how your experience and practice could be made available to encourage and inspire others.

In conclusion . . .

The spur for writing this book has been the evident mismatch between the established practice of organizing primary classrooms in groups and its half-forgotten rationale on the one hand and, on the other, the consistency of research evidence showing that the practices that best justify group seating are only infrequently used and that some alternative arrangements substantially benefit most children's ability to concentrate on individual tasks. The main pedagogical argument for sitting children in groups is eminently sensible: it is that the seating arrangement should support the learning activity. Small-group teaching and collaboration within groups of children justify grouped seating arrangements – when they are used. For other and, it turns out, more frequently used learning activities, other arrangements seem likely to be more effective. While existing research evidence on this is fairly persuasive, we need to be clear about its limitations for, at present, important questions about the relationships between different seating arrangements and the quality of teaching, learning, progress and attainment await investigation. What is clear already is the significantly detrimental consequence of the widespread practice of requiring young children to work in a context that does not match the most frequently encountered type of learning activity – individual work.

The fundamental case, therefore, is exactly the same as that used to justify group seating arrangements: the context should 'match' the activity. Putting this principle to work means that if children are to have different types of learning experience, different learning contexts will be needed. In rare circumstances, they might move between working areas set out for different activities, but most schools are not blessed with the space to allow this. The alternative is to stay in the same place and move the furniture to create the match. This is a feasible way of working, as the cases in Part 2 amply demonstrate, and, we are convinced, should become the established way of working across the primary school sector. For once, however, this is a decision that the teaching profession can make, not only on the basis of belief, but also informed by research evidence and by evaluating and disseminating classroom innovations within the profession.

References

Alexander, R. (1991) *Primary Education in Leeds: Twelfth and Final Report from the Primary Needs Independent Evaluation Project* (12). Leads: University of Leeds.

Alexander, R. (1992) *Policy and Practice in Primary Education.* London: Routledge.

Alexander, R. (1997) *Policy and Practice in Primary Education,* 2nd edn. London: Routledge.

Alexander, R. (2000) *Culture & Pedagogy: International Comparisons in Primary Education.* Oxford: Blackwell.

Alexander, R., Rose, J. and Woodhead, C. (1992) *Curriculum Organisation and Classroom Practice in Primary Schools: A Discussion Paper.* London: Department of Education and Science.

Axelrod, S., Hall, R. and Tams, S. (1979) Comparison of two common seating arrangements, *Academic Therapy, 15:* 29–36.

Bealing, D. (1972) Organisation of junior school classrooms, *Educational Research, 14:* 231–5.

Bennett, N. and Blundell, D. (1983) Quantity and quality of work in rows and classroom groups, *Educational Psychology, 3*(2): 93–105.

Bennett, N., Desforges, C., Cockburn, A. and Wilkinson, B. (1984) *The Quality of Pupil Learning Experiences.* London: Lawrence Erlbaum Associates.

Blatchford, P. and Kutnick, P. (1999) *The Nature and Use of Classroom Groups in Primary Schools: Final report* (R000237255). Swindon: Economic and Social Research Council.

Comber, C. and Wall, D. (2001) The classroom environment: a framework for learning, in C. Paechter, R. Edwards, R. Harrison and P. Twining (eds) *Learning, Space and Identity.* London: Paul Chapman.

Croll, P. (1996a) Teacher–pupil interaction in the classroom, in P. Croll and N. Hastings (eds) *Effective Primary Teaching: Research-based Classroom Strategies*. London: David Fulton.

Croll, P. (ed.) (1996b) *Teachers, Pupils and Primary Schooling: Continuity and Change*. London: Cassell.

Croll, P. and Moses, D. (1985) *One in Five: The Assessment and Incidence of Special Educational Needs*. London: Routledge & Keegan Paul.

Galton, M. and Patrick, H. (1990) *Curriculum Provision in Small Schools*. London: Routledge.

Galton, M. and Williamson, J. (1992) *Group Work in the Primary Classroom*. London: Routledge.

Galton, M., Simon, B. and Croll, P. (1980) *Inside the Primary Classroom*. London: Routledge & Keegan Paul.

Galton, M., Hargreaves, L. and Comber, C. (1998) Classroom practice and the National Curriculum in small rural primary schools, *British Educational Research Journal*, 24(1): 43–61.

Galton, M., Hargreaves, L., Comber, C., Wall, D. and Pell, A. (1999) *Inside the Primary Classroom: 20 Years On*. London: Routledge.

Gipps, C., McCallum, B. and Hargreaves, E. (2000) *What Makes a Good Primary School Teacher? Expert Classroom Strategies*. London: RoutledgeFalmer.

Hallam, S. and Ireson, J. (2001) Social inclusion and ability grouping in the primary school. Paper presented at the British Psychological Society Centenary Conference, Glasgow, April.

Hallam, S., Ireson, J., Chaudhury, I., Lister, V., Davies, J. and Mortimore, P. (1999) Ability grouping practices in the primary school: a survey of what schools are doing. Paper presented at the British Educational Reseach Association Conference, Brighton, September.

Hargreaves, L. (1990) Teachers and pupils in small schools, in M. Galton and H. Patrick (eds) *Curriculum Provision in the Small Primary School*, pp. 75–103. London: Routledge.

Hastings, N. (1998) Change and progress in primary teaching, in C. Richards and P. Taylor (eds) *How Shall We School Our Children? Primary Education and its Future*. London: Falmer Press.

Hastings, N. and Schwieso, J. (1995) Tasks and tables: the effects of seating arrangements on task engagement in primary schools, *Educational Research*, 37(3): 279–91.

Hastings, N., Schwieso, J. and Wheldall, K. (1996) A place for learning, in P. Croll and N. Hastings (eds) *Effective Primary Teaching: Research-based Classroom Strategies*. London: David Fulton.

Karweit, N. (1984) Time on-task reconsidered: synthesis of research on time and learning, *Educational Leadership*, 41: 32–5.

Kutnick, P. and Manson, I. (2000) Enabling children to learn in groups, in D. Whitebread (ed.) *The Psychology of Teaching and Learning in the Primary School*. London: RoutledgeFalmer.

McNamara, D.R. and Waugh, D.G. (1993) Classroom organisation: a discussion of grouping strategies in the light of the 'Three Wise Men's' report, *School Organisation*, 13(1): 41–50.

McPake, J., Harlen, W., Powney, J. and Davidson, J. (1999) *Teachers' and Pupils' Days in the Primary Classroom* (SCRE Research Report No. 93). Edinburgh: The Scottish Council for Research in Education.

Merrett, F. (1994) Whole class teaching and individualised approaches, in P. Kutnick and C. Rogers (eds) *Groups in Schools*. London: Cassell.

Mortimore, P., Sammons, P., Stoll, L., Lewis, D. and Ecob, R. (1988) *School Matters: The Junior Years*. London: Open Books.

Ofsted (Office for Standards in Education) (1998) *Setting in Primary Schools: A Report from Her Majesty's Chief Inspector of Schools*. London: Ofsted.

Ofsted (Office for Standards in Education) (2000) *Inspection Report on Long Lane Primary School, Tilehurst* (ref: 109853). London: Ofsted.

Osborn, M., McNess, E. and Broadfoot, P. (2000) *What Teachers Do: Changing Policy and Practice in Primary Education*. London: Continuum.

Plowden, B.H. (1967) *Children and their Primary Schools: a Report of the Central Advisory Council for Education (England)*, Vol. 1. London: HMSO.

Pollard, A., Broadfoot, P., Croll, P., Osborn, M. and Abbott, D. (1994) *Changing English Primary Schools?* London: Cassell.

Pollard, A., Triggs, P., Broadfoot, P., McNess, E. and Osborn, M. (2000) *What Pupils Say: Changing Policy and Practice in Primary Education*. London: Continuum.

Rosenfeld, P., Lambert, N.M. and Black, A. (1985) Desk arrangement effects on pupil classroom behaviour, *Journal of Educational Psychology*, 77(1): 101–8.

Tizard, B., Blatchford, P., Burke, J., Farquhar, C. and Plewis, I. (1988) *Young Children at School in the Inner City*. Hove: Lawrence Erlbaum Associates.

Topping, K. and Ehly, S. (eds) (1998) *Peer-Assisted Learning*. Mahwah, NJ: Lawrence Erlbaum Associates.

Wheldall, K. and Glynn, T. (1989) *Effective Classroom Learning*. Oxford: Blackwell.

Wheldall, K. and Lam, Y. (1987) Rows versus tables II: the effects of two classroom seating arrangements on disruption rates, on-task behaviour and teacher behaviour in three special school classes, *Educational Psychology*, 7(4), 303–12.

Wheldall, K., Morris, S., Vaughan, P. and Ng, Y. (1981) Rows versus tables: an example of behavioural ecology in two classes of eleven-year-old children, *British Journal of Educational Psychology*, 55(1): 51–63.

Wragg, E.C. (1993) *Primary Teaching Skills*. London: Routledge.

Yeomans, J. (1989) Changing seating arrangements: the use of antecedent control to increase on-task behaviour, *Behavioural Approaches with Children*, 13(3): 151–60.

Index

Note: page numbers in **bold** indicate diagrams or tables.